THE MAKING OF BRITAIN

The Middle Ages

THE MAKING OF BRITAIN

The Middle Ages

edited by

Lesley M. Smith

Schocken Books • New York

First American edition published by Schocken Books 1985
10 9 8 7 6 5 4 3 2 1   85 86 87 88
Copyright © London Weekend Television 1985
Published by agreement with Macmillan Publishers Ltd, London and Basingstoke

Library of Congress Cataloging in Publication Data
Main entry under title:
The Making of Britain.
   Bibliography: p.
   Includes index.
   1. Great Britain—History—Medieval period, 1066–
1485.   I. Smith, Lesley M.   II. Making of Britain
(Television program)
DA175.M34   1985   942   84-22185

Manufactured in Great Britain
ISBN 0-8052-3957-X

Contents

List of Maps and Illustrations

Acknowlegements

The publishers wish to acknowledge the following illustration sources:

The trustees of the British Museum; Foto Scala; Mr Leonard von Matt; Trinity College, Cambridge; The Dean and Chapter, Durham Cathedral; Tapisserie de Bayeux; Lutterworth Press; The Bodleian Library; John Freeman Photographic library; Woodmansterne Publications Ltd.; The Mansell Collection; Giraudon; Scottish Development Department; H.M. The Queen; National Library of Scotland; Scottish Record Office; Corpus Christi College, Cambridge; Scottish National Portrait Gallery; Cambridgeshire Record Office; Bibliothèque de Dijon; Society of Antiquaries; St John's College, Cambridge; Public Record Office; BBC Hulton Picture Library; The Dean and Chapter, Winchester Cathedral; The Honourable Society of the Inner Temple; National Maritime Museum.

Every effort has been made to trace all the copyright holders but if any have been inadvertently overlooked the publishers will be pleased to make the necessary arrangement at the first opportunity.

Preface

This volume is based on the second series of *The Making of Britain* produced by London Weekend Television. Once again I am grateful to all those at London Weekend Television involved in the series, Barry Cox, Mick Pilsworth and David Coulter, and to our commissioning editor at Channel Four, Naomi Sargeant. My thanks are due also to the contributors to the series and book, who generously shared their enthusiasm and expertise and, with great patience and tact, saved me from many errors. Other scholars shared their knowledge with me during the preparation of the series and this book, and I should like in particular to thank Professor Rodney Hilton and John Hatcher, who explained to me in great detail the workings of the medieval rural economy, and also Professor Geoffrey Barrow, Brenda Bolton, Elizabeth Hallam-Smith, Paul Hyams, Professor Henry Loyn, Michael Prestwich and Nigel Saul. I am grateful for the help and encouragement I received from our editor at Macmillan, Vanessa Peerless, while Pam Wilkinson, Jane Crush and Beverly Spurdens typed a difficult manuscript quickly and with great care.

L.M.S.
London, May 1984

Introduction

Lesley M. Smith

In the centuries after the fall of the Roman Empire, the nations of Britain that we know today gradually took shape. Attacked time after time by foreign invaders – Angles, Saxons, Scots, Norwegians and Danes – Britain in the eleventh century was stable and prosperous: stable, because both Scotland and England were united kingdoms governed by strong rulers; prosperous because it was part of a well-established and profitable trading empire which linked the Channel, the North Sea and the Baltic countries. In the middle of the eleventh century, this world was disrupted by the arrival, in the south of England, of a small army of French-speaking adventurers. They changed, as much by example as by conquest, the relationship between Britain and the rest of Europe.

In the traditional, and still widely-held, view of British history it was at this moment of conquest, as the last of the great Anglo-Saxon dynasties fell in battle to the army of an upstart foreign duke, William of Normandy, that the middle ages began. They then continued, punctuated with foreign battles and strewn with the corpses of murdered kings, until another battle at the end of the fifteenth century (this time at Bosworth, in the very heart of England) brought this turbulent period to a close. Here, in 1485, the last Yorkist king, Richard III, lost his throne, and his life, to a scheming Welshman, Henry Tudor, who was perhaps even more of an upstart than his Norman exemplar. In this analysis, a new man led Britain into a new age. This explanation of the middle ages is simple and seemingly logical: unfortunately, it is also wrong.

The very name 'middle ages' indicates that the conception is somewhat artificial. These centuries are defined in terms of what preceded them, the Dark Ages, or what succeeded them, the nationalist monarchy of the sixteenth century which culminated in the glorious reign of Elizabeth Tudor. Everything that happened during these centuries can be all too easily construed as a legacy of the past or a portent for the future.

Furthermore, while this neat division might have some use in English history, it has little or no relevance to the rest of Britain. For Wales, the final loss of independence to Edward I of England at the end of the thirteenth century is a break with the past far more dramatic than the outcome of a battle in southern England more than two hundred years earlier. Similarly, there is no natural break in Scottish history at, or even near, 1485. The real change in Scotland's historical horizons came with the Reformation, or with the transformation of James VI into a British king in 1603, or even in 1625 when Charles I, essentially an English king, tried to rule Scotland from Westminster.

Yet there is some truth in the traditional view. The reasons for change may be unconvincing, but change there was in Britain during the eleventh century, and at the end of the fifteenth century. But the roots of this change lie in Europe, not in the actions of the monarch who wore, usually unsteadily, the crown of England. It is in the expanding intellectual horizons and spiritual awakening of Europe that the making of Britain in the middle ages both begins and ends.

In the eleventh century, the nations which owed allegiance to the Christian church with its headquarters in Rome had a single identity. We might call it western Europe, but to contemporaries the most important aspect of this union was the common religious allegiance, and so it has been called instead western Christendom. These countries shared a common language, Latin, and were linked by a single organisation, the church. Inspired by the leaders of this church, these Christians took their message to the very edges of Europe and beyond – to pagan Scandinavia, and to the Moslem states of Spain and the Middle East. In the eleventh century, Britain belonged to this world, although isolated on its far western frontier. What the Norman conquest did was to accelerate Britain's full-scale involvement. This was as true of Scotland, where there was no invasion, and no change from a native to a Norman dynasty, as it was of England. But it was the work of more than a hundred years, not a single day on the battlefield in 1066. This mood of self-confident, aggressive expansion recurred in the fifteenth century. Europe turned its attention first to the distant nations of the known world – India, China and Africa – then, at the very end of the fifteenth century, to the hitherto unknown continent of America. As men's attention shifted westwards from the Mediterranean and its links with the east to the Atlantic and the continent beyond, Britain (ironically through little effort of its own), was transformed from an island on the edge of the known world into a group of nations set at the very centre of a new world, and a new, transatlantic economy. This, more than any change of dynasty in England, was to shape Britain's history for the next three hundred years.

W. L. Warren and Geoffrey Parker both take the expansion of Europe as their theme and show how the difference between the two ages of European expansion was more than one of distance and perspective. Inspired in the eleventh century by religious fervour, Europe's adventurers in the fifteenth century faced the unknown with one over-riding aim – the accumulation of wealth. Holy armies, blessed by the pope, were the instruments of expansion in the eleventh century. Four centuries later, a few sea-borne merchant adventurers, viewed as eccentrics by most of their contemporaries, accepted the most outlandish geographical ideas of the day and used the untried technology of navigation to thread their way unsteadily around the world. Perhaps most importantly, the leadership for the expansion of the eleventh century came from the holy city of Rome, and drew on men's allegiance to the ideal of a united Christendom. The expansion of the fifteenth century was the work of the nations of the Iberian peninsula – Portugal and Spain – obscure, poor, and only recently fully liberated from the rule of pagan Arabs.

Here lies the evidence for what was probably the most important cultural and intellectual change of the middle ages – the decline in the power and authority of the universal church and a parallel rise in the confidence and capability of individual rulers, and the people whom they ruled. Anne Duggan, Michael Clanchy and David Carpenter all analyse different aspects of this intellectual history, showing how it engendered a new, critical self-awareness among the educated and literate laity of the late fifteenth century.

In a society where both kings and popes claimed supreme authority in the state, there were bound to be struggles for power. Throughout the twelfth century, the papacy was in the ascendant, rallying the soldiers and kings of Europe under its banner and inspiring a sweeping renaissance in thought and spirituality that found physical expression in the art and architecture of churches, cathedrals and monasteries all over Europe.

But the European nations of the thirteenth century, particularly France and England, were much more introverted, concerned with the realities of power and politics in north western Europe, not with the misplaced ideals of churchmen. When Louis IX of France and Frederick II, the German emperor, went on crusade, they dreamed of creating a new empire around the eastern shores of the Mediterranean, not of recreating the kingdom of God on earth. By the end of the century this secular spirit had triumphed. Philip IV of France forced the pope to abandon much of his authority over the French clergy and church. In the first decade of the fourteenth century, the popes were forced out of Rome by the bitter civil wars raging throughout Italy and driven to take refuge at Avignon, under the protection of the same Philip IV and his successors. The papacy now had to come to terms with the realities of late medieval politics, and recognise its own dependence on the power of friendly kings. The final blow came seventy years later, when rivalries within the organisation of the church itself led to the election of two (and at one point, three) popes. Each had his own adherents among the nations of Europe, but the choice was determined by political needs not by theological niceties. The ideal of a united western Christendom was truly dead.

The new focus for men's loyalty and aspirations was the king, and a more abstract idea, the nation. Prolonged wars between the European states helped to foster this feeling, but it was re-inforced by the growth of national languages, which began to replace Latin as the medium of written, as well as spoken communication. When ruler and ruled shared the same language, they also shared a common identity and a common future, which in turn gave men a greater confidence not only in politics but in every aspect of their daily lives. Again, people's attitude to religion is a telling example of changes in intellectual attitudes. Although the church had failed to keep alive the ideal of a Christendom united in peace under its leadership, it had managed to project the ideal of a truly religious life lived in imitation of Christ to many people all over Europe. In so doing it had furnished at least the literate and educated among its congregations with a standard against which they could measure the performance of the church. In the fourteenth and fifteenth centuries, many, like the Flemish mystic, Gerhard Groote or John Wycliffe, an English teacher, turned away from the church, advocating a direct, personal relationship with God as the best, if not the only, route to salvation. This was a very important shift in perspective, for if the individual could take responsibility for what was still the most important aspect of life – his fate after death – he could certainly read books for himself, educate his children and sail the Atlantic in search of new worlds.

But the making of Britain in the middle ages cannot be explained solely in European terms, however important they may be. What happened in Britain is just as important as the changing world around Britain. But there are difficulties in writing a truly British history of the middle ages. The great historians of the late nineteenth century, who in a sense founded the academic study of history as we know it today, have left behind them a rather awkward legacy. First of all, writers like Bishop Stubbs, Regius professor of history in the university of Oxford in the 1880s, were looking into Britain's distant history at exactly the same time as Britain not only ruled an empire which spanned the globe, but also appeared to have brought to that empire a share in its own triumphant civilisation. Naturally, these historians believed that limited parliamentary democracy and the ancient legal system which guaranteed the freedom of every honest man were the sources of Britain's national character, and its international success. As both these institutions had their origins in the middle ages, they quickly made the assumption that Britain – in particular England – was far more advanced (in nineteenth century terms) much earlier than any other European nation. Secondly, the complicated evolution of Britain as a political entity emphasised this anglo-centric view. It was the English parliament at Westminster to which Wales, Scotland and Ireland eventually sent representatives. It was English law that administrators took to America in the seventeenth century, to Australia in the eighteenth, to India and Africa in the nineteenth century. This has encouraged historians to view England as a sophisticated constitutional pathbreaker, with much of our history being the efforts of the rest of Britain to catch up with this democratic ideal.

John Gillingham, Chris Given-Wilson and Alexander Grant all look behind the smokescreen of Victorian prejudice and demonstrate that the traditional milestones of the British constitution – Magna Carta, the admittance of the commons to a share of power in parliament – were nothing more than pragmatic responses, on both sides of the conflict, to short-term crises in the functioning of royal government. They were never intended as permanent definitions of the balance of power between the king and his subjects, but once created, they were impossible to destroy. In medieval terms they limited the king's power and in the long run made the good government they were designed to ensure much more difficult to achieve. When the crises, caused mainly by the enormous cost of foreign war and the humiliation of defeat, were absent, as in Scotland, so too were the institutions and the artificial limitations on the king's power. In medieval terms this was good government, and the definition of rule by democratic consent as the 'correct' way for a British king to govern was still more than two centuries in the future.

In the last instance, history is about people, and the remaining chapters in the book build up a picture of the way people lived, worked and died in medieval Britain. Land was the basis of everyone's life, from the king down to the poorest peasant, and so David Carpenter and Caroline Barron survey the two sides of life on the land: the long, relentless toil of the peasant on the one hand, and the leisured, cultured family life of the landlords on the other. John Post delves into legal records to try and cast a little more light on the daily lives of these people, who often leave no memorial beyond the date of their birth and death, and a bare record of their appearance before the King's judges. Finally, Richard Mackenney analyses the very special conditions that fostered the growth of towns, and began to draw people away from this rural world into the profitable commercial life protected by the walls of Britain's towns.

These chapters also show how the landscape of Britain, particularly rural Britain, was created in the middle ages. Quite apart from the cathedrals and the castles that attract thousands of visitors every year, it was in the middle ages that the forests were cleared, and the new land was broken, which turned lowland England and Scotland into rich agricultural countries. Villages that still exist today grew up around monasteries, cross-roads and markets; towns founded in the middle ages have survived, though with varying fortunes, until the present day, while even the 'new' towns of the nineteenth and twentieth centuries have often been built around the nucleus of a medieval village. Village churches, royal castles, even the names of streets, all recall the middle ages, when the Britain so familiar to us today was shaped by the ambitions of kings and lords and the toil of those who laboured on the land.

CHAPTER ONE

The Outer Edge of the Earth

W.L. Warren

At the time of the Norman Conquest of England, at the time of the First Crusade, how did people picture the world to themselves? We can answer this question from the many schematised maps which survive in medieval manuscripts. Shown overleaf is a fine example from an eleventh century commentary on the Book of Revelation.[1] Like all such maps it has the Mediterranean in the middle of the world landmass. That, of course, is what 'Mediterranean' means – from the Latin words *medius*, 'the middle', and *terra*, 'land'. Europe lies to the left, Africa to the right, and Asia is at the top. In many ways this is a surprisingly knowledgeable map. It shows how the inland sea reaches beyond the Hellespont. It knows about the Caspian Sea and the deserts which lie beyond. It knows about the Red Sea and the Persian Gulf. It knows about Mesopotamia and Persia and India. It identifies the furthest reaches of the conquests of Alexander the Great in Bactria. Somewhere up there, it believes, lies the Garden of Eden. This conception of the world has an elegant symmetry. Observe the mountain ranges, and how the rivers flow either inward towards the central sea, or outward towards the encircling ocean at the edge of the world. So what we have is a neatly counterbalancing, intellectually satisfying conception with, at the centre of creation, the city of Jerusalem, which St Jerome had described as the umbilical cord which connects the earthly life with the divine.[2]

Unfortunately symmetry has limitations when trying to fit the known world into a coherent scheme. There are bits, as it were, left over; and one of the most awkward bits, for it was too large and well-known to be ignored, was the British Isles. It had to be fitted in on the outer edge of the world, and on this map it curves like a long sausage around the coast of France, with Ireland butting up against Spain.

English writers tended to be somewhat defensive about Britain's

1.1. An eleventh century map of the world

1.2. A mosaic showing the Holy City of Jerusalem

location at the outer edge of civilisation, insisting that it was nevertheless well-endowed with God's bounty, and hinting that it might be marked out for a special destiny.[3] There were, however, many people living at the time who knew that the facts of geography did not fit this intellectual world-conception. They had to use more realistic route maps when they journeyed to Rome, or made their way to the famous shrine of St James at Compostella in Spain, or navigated the Baltic. This world map was not the real world. This was the world as it ought to be. This is a map in the mind.

Intellectually, this view of the world linked medieval scholars to what they had read of classical antiquity, and to the world of St Paul and St Augustine. At the same time it shows us how, to them, Christendom seemed hemmed in by heretics and infidels. It makes us realise why, when Pope Urban II in 1095 called for volunteers from western Europe to go to the help of Christians in the east, it was interpreted as a call to liberate Jerusalem from the clutches of Islam.

Yet the odd fact is that when the First Crusade set out, Jerusalem had been in the hands of the Moslems for over four hundred years, and no one had thought of such a venture before. Crusading zeal for the expulsion of the infidel was something quite new in the eleventh century and it was profoundly shocking to native Christians and Moslems of the Near East who for generations had learned to live together in mutual respect.[4] Attitudes among western Christians, both in the theology of war and in popular piety, were undergoing fundamental change. One aspect of it is a shift in devotional emphasis in western Christianity from the Resurrection to the Crucifixion. We can see this in the way that Christ is portrayed. Traditionally Christ had been shown in triumph over sin and death, wearing the crown and robes of the King of Heaven. But the new image which emerges in the eleventh century and which comes to dominate western piety for centuries was that of Christ broken and suffering on the Cross. This is more than a mere change of fashion. It is one sign of a widespread, far-reaching and astonishing break with tradition in western Europe in

1.3. Christ on the Cross

the eleventh century. The justification for it was a missionary zeal to set the world to rights, and to focus men's minds on what was thought to be God's will. These Jerusalem-centred maps are part of this intellectual justification. Interestingly they start to appear at the end of the eleventh century and become popular in the twelfth just when, in fact, the ancient notion of a Mediterranean-based world was becoming an anachronism.

The Roman Empire of antiquity had become partitioned into three power-blocs, three spheres of influence, three religious offiliations. They can be identified by the language in which their religion was expressed: Greek, Arabic, or Latin. For centuries the Greek-speaking and Arabic-speaking power-blocs had been the arbiters of the known world. At the beginning of the eleventh century they were still the dominant super-powers, but by the end of the eleventh century they had lost control of their own destinies. Latin-speaking Europe was stepping onto the stage of world history.

Sophisticated easterners were aghast when they encountered Latin Christians on the First Crusade. Anna Comnena, daughter of the Byzantine emperor, portrayed them as uncouth, aggressive, arrogant, and ignorant.[5] She was right. But they were also adventurous, dynamic, and self-confident. The self-confidence was something new; it was part of the break with tradition; the hitherto backward west was no longer content to borrow from its betters; it was moving from imitation to innovation.

Latin Christendom was expanding in the eleventh century. It was challenging Constantinople for the religious allegiance of the Slavs. It was reaching out to Scandinavia. It was rolling back Islam in Spain. Rome itself was becoming something more than merely the 'mother church' of Latin Christendom, the resort of pilgrims seeking out relics in the catacombs and a blessing from the patriarchal figure who sat on the throne of St Peter. The holy city was becoming the headquarters of an ecclesiastical organisation which confidently assumed a divine mandate for the direction of the world.[6] The bishops of Rome still tended to think in Mediterranean terms. They wanted the orthodox churches of the eastern Mediterranean to acknowledge their authority, and in launching the crusades to the Holy Land they were trying to seize control of the Christian heartland. But the papacy was much less Italian in character than it had been and the impulses which moved it were coming, for the first time in history, from north of the Alps.

The balance of power in the Western world was shifting decisively away from the Mediterranean to the countries north of the Alps. This was a long drawn-out process; but it was gathering irresistible momentum by the late eleventh century. It is easier to illustrate than explain, but part of the reason is undoubtedly a new prosperity in northern Europe. The underlying factor was an improvement in the climate. This, of course, is difficult to measure without records and statistics, but we can read the signs. For example, the Alpine glaciers retreated further than they have ever done. The level of the sea rose on the Frisian coasts. Norsemen could colonise Greenland and Labrador. The weather, it seems, was generally a little warmer and much drier.[7] This helped northern Europe more than the south which tended to become too dry.[8] Growing vines to make decent wine spread further north than at any time between the Roman Empire and the present day. But much more important, grain production improved dramatically in quality and quantity: bread grains, beer grains, and feed grains – the staple foods of men and horses. It was in the eleventh century that the countries of the twentieth century EEC started producing their first agricultural surpluses.

Moreover, for the first time since plague had ravaged the later Roman Empire, the population of Europe was increasing, and was to go on increasing until plague struck again in the fourteenth century.[9] This, too, is hard to measure but again there are signs to be read. Urban populations which had for centuries huddled forlornly in a corner of an old walled Roman city suddenly expanded, filling the walled area and tumbling out into suburbs. The old city of York doubled in size; Tournai in Flanders trebled. In Germany new towns gathered around markets where none had been before. Norwich, a largish village in the tenth century, had become a major town with twenty-five churches by the time of Domesday Book (1086).[10] Many old churches had to be rebuilt, partly because they were no longer large enough and partly because the simple barn-like structures of old were no longer deemed worthy enough. The contemporary French chronicler, Raoul Glaber, wrote that 'the world was casting off its old rags to reclothe itself in the white robes of churches'. The spate of church building was, he thought, one of the most striking features of his day; another was the frequency of travellers on the road, and most surprising of all, for it was something quite new, the large number of women pilgrims.[11]

Population growth sustained other dramatic changes. Northern Europe had been, quite literally, the backwoods of the Roman Empire. But now a start was made on systematically clearing the primeval woodland. It was laborious, back-breaking work; but as more fertile land was brought into cultivation, more families could rear more children, who in turn could clear more of the forest.[12] An increasing population provided not only the justification for rebuilding cathedrals and monasteries but also the huge force of manual labourers required for the work. It sent younger sons off to seek their fortune in new lands, to apprentice themselves to a trade or to seek an education

1.4. Knights on crusade

in the schools. It manned the crusades and started northern Europe's first overseas colonies – in the Holy Land. Strikingly, the common language of the crusader colonies was northern French – the *lingua franca* (as ever since we have termed a form of international common speech); and the Turks always knew the crusaders as 'the Franks'.

The new prosperity did not simply happen. Climate may have been an underlying factor which made an agricultural revolution in parts of Europe possible, but it was not a cause. Peasants living at subsistence level do not change their farming habits simply because life gets a little easier. Arable farming geared to large-scale grain production for the market required major capital resources in terms of equipment, manpower and animal-power. Even to put together a plough team of eight oxen required several peasant families to pool their resources. An agricultural revolution on this scale involved relocating scattered peasant households into village communities managing large arable fields by co-operative effort. In the process, the settlement pattern and landscape of northern Europe were reshaped. The impetus came from rulers and landlords mobilising resources to wage their wars, but success depended on the extent to which they could win or enforce the co-operation of the peasants. The new, well-organised socio-economic unit by which the land was more effectively exploited was, of course, what is commonly known as 'the manor'. We may think of it as principally for the benefit of the landlord, but it was also, in economic terms, the medieval equivalent of the soviet collective farm or the Israeli kibbutz. People were forced to live and work by strict rules but at the same time they were offered greater security.

Making the most of the new possibilities required discipline and organisation, which did not come easily to a Europe notorious for disorder; but those who trained themselves to it reaped the reward of success. 'Discipline' and 'organisation' became the watchwords of a new western ideology. One sign of it is the way that monasteries, instead of being separate communities became organised into monastic 'orders'.[13] Another is that the most respected rulers were no longer those with the greatest prestige but those who ruthlessly imposed law and order. We may detect it in the eleventh century belief in a specialisation within society – of a division into those who labour, those who fight, and those who pray.[14]

One of the most striking features of eleventh century Europe was a new kind of alliance between the fighting-men and the praying-men. Monks were no longer simply to seek the salvation of their own souls: they were expected to intercede with the Almighty for the society in which they lived. In the early middle ages it had been common for rulers to retire to a monastery, to cast aside the cares of the world and repent of the sinful life they had led, before death claimed them; but now rulers were told to get on with the job of ruling and leave their souls to the care of the monks (in return, of course, for their benefactions). Monks themselves went out in the world, to preach and advise, and to become bishops, popes, and statesmen. Their special quality was that they were men trained to discipline and organisation. It was they who persuaded the fighting-men to turn their energies away from internecine warfare to fighting the enemies of the church and to become 'soldiers of Christ'.[15]

Those fighting men who most successfully took over the management of the new Europe were those who learned a new kind of organised, disciplined warfare. For generations men had been looking for better ways of using horses in warfare. The most effective was that developed in north-west Europe: the heavily armoured cavalry of a specialised military élite – the *chivalers* or 'knights'. Knights were the battle tanks of medieval armies. Horses and riders had to co-operate in battle formations instead of showing off their individual prowess, for the heavy cavalry's success lay in the co-ordinated charge.[16] As the Turks said, a Frankish charge could bash a hole in the walls of Babylon.[17]

Knights were highly efficient. A few well-trained, properly equipped knights could do the job of hundreds of foot soldiers. No longer did armies have to pillage the land like swarms of locusts. But knights

1.5. The equipment of a
knight

1.6. The seal of William
the Lion, King of Scots

were expensive to equip and maintain. The essential coat of mail cost the equivalent of a family farm. The specially bred, carefully trained warhorse was worth a ransom. Knights indeed could be supported only on the disciplined, productive labour of manorialised peasants. The agricultural revolution was essential to the military revolution.

The predominance of the knight in the new European society may be illustrated in two ways. First, monk and knight fused in the crusading military orders of the Knights Hospitaller and Templar – a striking expression of the sanctified militarism of Latin Christendom. Secondly, the code of the *chivalers*, the cult of chivalry, became the ethos not simply of the fighting men but of the ruling class as a whole. It is striking how, from the late eleventh century, kings themselves were portrayed on their seals on horseback, wearing the accoutrements and bearing the weapons of the knight.

Not everyone, however, immediately favoured the new techniques of heavy cavalry. Aristocratic warlords took a pride in traditional skills. It was the *nouveaux riches* (such as the dukes of Normandy) who adopted this new-fangled cavalry. The élite troops of the German monarchy were pre-eminent at fighting on foot with great swords. The élite troops of the English monarchy also fought on foot, but had adopted the Viking battle-axe. Both of those traditional military élites went down to relatively small cavalry forces of Normans – the Germans, fighting for the pope, at Civitate in 1053, the English at Hastings in 1066.[18]

The emergence of the Normans as a powerful force changing the direction of European history was astonishingly swift. Normandy got its name from the 'Northmen' who had seized control in the early tenth century, but little trace of Viking influence remained by the middle of the eleventh. There had been a vicious internal struggle for power which had turned into a revolution. The losers had to seek their fortunes elsewhere, taking service as mercenaries in southern Italy, and then, by ruthless opportunism, taking over there. The victors – 'new' men mostly with short pedigrees – entrenched themselves as enthusiastic exponents of the newest techniques of warcraft and statecraft, and embraced with evangelical fervour the 'modern' gospel of disciplined, God-fearing, militarism. They paid well to buy the best expertise available, recruiting the ablest knights wherever they could be found, and bringing in the keenest reforming monks from as far away as Burgundy and northern Italy. They sought to ensure that God would be on their side by founding more than twenty-five new monasteries; and they built them in a grander, bolder style than ever seen before to let God know they were on his side. Scholars and students from far and wide flocked to the monastic schools in Normandy, including Anselm of Lucca, the future Pope Alexander II

1.7. The Norman
monastery at Jumièges

(who was to give papal blessing to Norman military enterprises) and
two other Italians whose careers under Norman patronage were to
culminate as successive archbishops of Canterbury.[19] What is
striking is not simply the success of the Normans but also the
international character of the culture they embraced, and the constant
interchange of men and ideas right across Europe from the Adriatic to
the English Channel. There is little sign, however, that this culture
had much influence across the English Channel.

The critical question for England in the later eleventh century was
whether it wished to be a part of this new Europe. England had

benefited richly from the improved climate and the agricultural revolution; and in its long wars against the Danes had learned how best to mobilise resources and maximise profits. Now that the wars were over, it overflowed with wealth. London was an international trading station – the entrepôt for the North Sea and Baltic trades (which Danish kings were trying to monopolise). King Cnut (1016–35) negotiated a commercial treaty with the rulers of northern Italy to reduce the delays on English traders passing through the customs posts at the Alpine passes.[20] But trade seems to be about the limit of English interest in the mainland.

Eleventh century England was introverted – understandably so, for the union of Anglo-Saxons and Danes into a united kingdom passed through a period of stresses and strains, and ended in a hard-won compromise and merger. It is reflected in the blending of Scandinavian elements into the English language. English adapted Scandinavian pronouns; Anglo-Saxon borrowed such convenient forms as *take up* and *put down*; it came to speak of *laws* instead of *dooms*, of a *window*, instead of an *eye-thurl* (i.e. 'wind-eye' instead of 'eye hole'), of *wrong* instead of *unright*; it embraced identical terms such as *ugly* and *unfair* and gave them different meanings; it took over and made its own such everyday words as *skin* and *skull*, *bull* and *kid*, *axle* and *keel*, *steak* and *egg*, *knife* and *sky*, *awkward*, *happy*, and *weak*.[21] Here we may see the final reconciliation and the emergence of a common culture.

The reconciliation brought back an Englishman to the throne of England after the rule of the Danish King Cnut and his sons. He was King Edward the Confessor (1042–66). He had spent much of his youth in exile in Normandy – his mother's home, and the place where his cousins ruled. He brought Normans to England and showed them favour. They were deeply unpopular. One, given an earldom in the west midlands, put his English troops on horseback and led them to disaster against the Welsh. Cavalry warfare was not for novices, and in the circumstances it was not surprising that the English thought they knew best how to manage their own affairs. In 1052 many of the king's Norman friends were expelled. Yet the Normans of Normandy had originally been Vikings spilling over from the invasion of England. The fact that they now seemed unutterably 'foreign' is an indication of how 'Frenchified' they had become, and how they had adjusted to the changes sweeping Europe. The English Channel had become a cultural divide.

In 1066 when Edward the Confessor died childless, the Anglo-Danish realm had an open choice of claimants to the throne. Was it to opt for the new Europe and accept the late king's kinsman, Duke William of Normandy? Or was it to opt for the Scandinavian heirs of King Cnut and stay with the outer rim of the world? Significantly it opted for neither, but sought instead to keep itself to itself by choosing the late king's brother-in-law – a man who symbolised the union that constituted the kingdom of England: an Englishman who had a Danish mother and a Scandinavian name, Harold, Earl of Wessex.

Unfortunately for King Harold, the kingdom of England was too tempting a prize for those who thought they had a better claim. The king of Norway and the king of Denmark hankered after recreating the North Sea empire of King Cnut. Duke William of Normandy thought that the wealth of England could buy him enough knights to make Normandy the dominant power in northern France. The king of Norway was the first on the scene and the forgotten encounter of 1066 was the epic battle at Stamford Bridge. Of the three hundred ships which had brought the Norwegians up the Humber, only twenty-four were needed to carry away the survivors. Three days later Duke William risked all on a night-time crossing of the Channel and landed at Pevensey Bay. King Harold brought his army down from the north by forced marches, covering two hundred and forty miles, and stood ready to meet William on a hill near Hastings. He would have done better to have bided his time. For a whole day, on 14 October 1066, the old way of warfare struggled with the new. The new won – but only just.[22]

The battle of Hastings gave Duke William the crown, but it did not give him the kingdom. To his surprise and chagrin he had to fight for that piece by piece. The Norman conquest of England did not take place suddenly in 1066 but bitterly between 1068 and 1075. It was

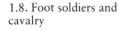
1.8. Foot soldiers and cavalry

not a mass migration of colonists looking for lands to settle. It was a campaign waged by a few thousand professional warriors – men who lived by war and expected it to yield a profit. Williams's barons took shares in the enterprise not because he commanded them to go to war, but freely investing their resources, their expertise, and the skills of their knights in expectation of establishing a branch of the family estate-business across the Channel.

It had the character of a commercial venture – a take-over bid for a long-established, prestigious, and profitable business, whose management had grown a little too complacent. William intended to shake up the running of the business, cream off the surplus profits, and strip the assets. The battle of Hastings put William's men on the board of directors, but it did not in fact give them effective control. They were challenged by shareholder revolts, workforce strikes, and attempts by regions to opt out of the new system. In consequence William had to divide among his barons the task of seizing possession of all the assets, ousting the English owner-managers, and putting in trustworthy Normans. The famous Domesday Book was a vast inventory made in

1.9. Reconstruction of a motte and bailey castle

1086 of the profitable resources of England, and showing who among the Normans had gained control of the land.[23]

One dramatic sign of the take-over was something quite new on the landscape of England – the castle. It might be a great stone fortress which the king or his barons built as the imposing regional headquarters of the new administration, or one of the numerous stockaded forts which the knights erected in the countryside to protect their families and servants from the hostility of the natives.[24] Another sign of total take-over was the disappearance of English as the language of government and of the upper levels of society, within five years of Hastings. The new bosses spoke French and wrote Latin. When, generations later, English re-emerged, it had picked up elements of French. Commonly they were words to do with government – like *government* itself, and *justice, judge,* and *jury, court, prison, tax, mayor. Money* too is French; and although the English institution of 'king' survived, his power was *royal*.[25]

Some of the old English ruling class were depressed to the level of the peasantry. Many emigrated. Some trekked right across Europe to Constantinople and enlisted in the emperor's bodyguard. They found themselves fighting Normans again – the Normans who had defeated the pope's army at Civitate, who had captured Sicily, and were beavering away at the edges of the Byzantine empire (yet another example of the eruption of northern Europe into the Mediterranean).[26] The one surviving member of the English royal house, Edgar Atheling, was last heard of commanding a Byzantine naval squadron which went to help the First Crusade in desperate straits at Antioch.[27]

The English, like the Byzantines, may have resented the Normans as cocky upstarts; but the Normans, for their part, did not hide their scorn for English provincial backwardness.[28] In less than a generation they had pulled down every Anglo-Saxon cathedral and abbey and most of the churches too, and had rebuilt them on a much bigger scale, in the Norman version of 'modern' architecture.[29] Even at the time this was questioned as an unnecessary, arrogant extravagance.[30] On the other hand we should remember that the new Durham cathedral was the most advanced, daring and exciting building in Europe, a symbol of what the Normans achieved in England.

Having overwhelmed England, the Normans filtered into Scotland (invited by a faction among the Scots to modernise its monarchy). They burrowed into Wales (as private enterprise take-over bidders) and, a century after Hastings, they spilled over into Ireland. So it happened that they linked together all parts of the British Isles and hitched them to continental Europe. Here too – as in the Holy Land – northern French was the *lingua franca*.

1.10. The cathedral and castle at Durham, dominating the city

Further Reading

C.M. Cipolla (ed.), *The Fontana Economic History of Europe: The Middle Ages* (London, 1972); M.T. Clanchy, *England and its Rulers, 1066–1272* (London, 1983); R.H.C. Davis, *The Normans and their Myth* (London, 1976); D.C. Douglas, *The Norman Achievement, 1050–1100* (London, 1969); S. Runciman, *A History of the Crusades* (Cambridge, 1951); R.W. Southern, *The Making of the Middle Ages* (London, 1953).

The New Europeans

Anne Duggan

About the year 1100 a young cleric, Adelard of Bath, left England on a lifetime of study and travel. His goal was the treasury of classical Greek learning, all but lost with the fall of the western Roman Empire in the mid-fifth century, which Islamic scholars working in Bukhara and Cordoba in the ninth and tenth centuries had translated into Arabic. His voyage of discovery took him to Asia Minor, Italy, Sicily and Christian Spain – wherever there was the chance of acquiring new texts or meeting the scholars who were either skilled in Arabic and Greek, the languages which could unlock the desired riches, or who were proficient in the new learning. By 1120 he had learned enough Arabic to make the first Latin translation of the geometrical works of Euclid. Adelard was one of the first of the wandering scholars of the twelfth century whose thirst for knowledge led them to the religious and intellectual frontiers of their time. They travelled to acquire mastery of Latin, the international language of law, learning and administration; they sought the powerful methods of argumentation contained in Aristotle's logic; and they sought the advanced principles of law and jurisprudence contained in the classical law of the Roman Empire and in the emerging law of the Western Church. In short, they travelled to acquire the knowledge which would fit them for office in the church or service in the rapidly expanding bureaucracy of the state.

The Norman Conquest had brought many changes to England, not least of which were the introduction of a French-speaking aristocracy in church and state and the joining of the island kingdom to the duchy of Normandy. This French connection was reinforced in 1154 when Henry I's grandson, Henry of Anjou, succeeded Stephen as king and so linked England and Normandy with extensive territories in the west and south-west of France, thus creating the Angevin Empire. As count

2.1. Medieval Islamic scholars at work in a library

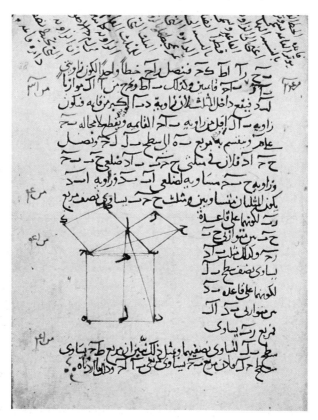

2.2. A page from an arabic translation of Euclid

of Anjou, Maine and Touraine, count of Poitou, duke of Normandy and duke of Aquitaine, Henry II (1154–89) ruled more of France than the French king. From being on the periphery of Europe, England became a European power with European interests, more closely bound to the continent than ever before. The marriage alliances of Henry II's children demonstrate the cosmopolitan outlook very clearly. His three daughters married Henry the Lion of Saxony, Alfonso III of Castile, and William II of Sicily; three of his sons married respectively Margaret of France, Constance of Brittany, and Berengaria of Navarre. Only the youngest son, John 'lackland', was provided with a wife closer to home in Isabella of Gloucester, whom he later abandoned for Isabelle, heiress of the county of Angoulême. These marriages reflect the international ambitions and preoccupations of the English monarchy, and the wider horizons opened up to Englishmen.

This reorientation could hardly have occurred at a more fortunate time. The two centuries from 1050 to 1250 were a period of general resurgence in all aspects of European life – intellectual, religious, aesthetic and political – in an environment of urban renewal and economic expansion, characterised by an internationalism, a confidence, and a dynamism unknown since the fall of the Roman Empire. During this period, Christendom was able to reverse the previously inexorable advance of Islam into the countries around the Mediterranean, and create an economic and cultural community capable of challenging the domination of the Moslem world. The Christian reconquest of Spain from 1031 (Toledo was captured in 1085) and the crusading movement from 1095 are aspects of the growing Christian confidence in the face of Islam.

This confidence was sustained by an unexampled economic expansion. Population trebled, cultivation extended to the limits of agrarian capacity, town life revived, industry and commerce expanded, and Italian merchants established the foundations of international credit and banking. New trade brought new wealth; and new wealth, in the hands of manufacturers, merchants and bankers, began to challenge the agrarian-based power of the landed aristocracy. Henry II of England, for example, borrowed regularly from William Cade (as well as from the Jews), and by the mid-thirteenth century, Italian bankers (from Milan, Florence and Siena) provided credit facilities for kings, popes and princes. Though less spectacularly than Italian or Flemish cities, English towns like London, Norwich, York and Northampton grew rapidly in population, wealth and influence.

Six major commodities – English wool, Flemish and French cloth (the green cloth of Arras and the scarlet cloth of Brabant fetched more than cloth of gold in the European markets), oriental luxuries and spices (silk, pearls, ivory, pepper, nutmeg), Italian brocades, Gascon wine and Sicilian corn – were transported across the waterways of Europe to the trade fairs of Champagne at Lagny, Bar-sur-Aube, Troyes and Provins. Trade routes by land and sea linked the Mediterranean with India and China; the world of commerce stretched to the frontiers of the known world. The geographical boundaries of Europe were broken down, and missionaries and merchants travelled to the ends of the earth. By the 1280s Marco Polo was serving Kublai Khan in China; by the 1290s John of Monte Corvino (*c.* 1254–1324) was establishing the first Christian mission in Khanbalik (Peking), where he was appointed archbishop in 1307.

Against this background, the mental and religious horizons of Europe were enlarged by the creation of new institutions of higher education, by the revival of Roman and canon law, and by the progressive assimilation of classical learning. These changes amounted to an intellectual revolution as important in its consequences as the Italian renaissance of the fifteenth century or the scientific revolution of the seventeenth. Hitherto, higher learning had been largely confined to monastic schools, where a classical pattern of education based on the *trivium* and the *quadrivium* had been established as the foundation of theological study. The *trivium* provided the basic literary skills of Latin grammar, rhetoric (or style) and logic; the *quadrivium* comprised the practical skills of arithmetic, geometry, astronomy and music. Together, they constituted the seven liberal arts. By means of this programme of elementary education, the knowledge of a limited number of Latin works (like Priscian's *Grammar*) and of Latin translations of Greek works, mostly by the sixth century Boethius (*c.* 480–524) survived through the early middle ages as a link with the intellectual culture of the classical past which could provide a springboard for future development.

The impetus for change came from two directions simultaneously. From the last quarter of the eleventh century, the demands of the ecclesiastical reform movement for an educated clergy fostered the expansion of education outside the monasteries, and the most advanced learning moved to the more challenging and dynamic atmosphere of urban and cathedral schools. Here the teaching techniques of lecture and commentary were perfected, the knowledge inherited from the past was subjected to searching critical analysis by the sharpest minds of the time, and Roman and canon law were established as major subjects alongside the traditional study of theology and the liberal arts.

Meanwhile, the Christian reconquest of Spain, the Norman conquests of Apulia and Sicily, and the Venetian commercial expansion into Asia Minor, established contacts with the Arab world

2.3. Centres of learning in the twelfth century

2.4. Hugh of St Victor teaching

and with Byzantium – with the two civilisations which had preserved the cultural achievements of the ancient Greeks. Of these, it was the Arab contacts, especially in Sicily and Spain, which proved the more fruitful, since Moslem scholars had made their own distinct contribution to the advancement of mathematics, astronomy, medicine and philosophy, and Latin scholars came into contact with a living intellectual tradition which in some respects surpassed their own. The intellectual enlightenment, loosely called the twelfth century renaissance, grew from the fusion between the Christian scholasticism already flourishing in the urban and cathedral schools in France and Italy and the new learning in mathematics, science and philosophy which gradually percolated into the mainstream of European culture throughout the twelfth and thirteenth centuries. But we should not exaggerate the dependence of the Latins on Arab learning. The dynamic movement in theology and law was already under way in Paris, Laon, Bologna and elsewhere before the new learning was introduced, and the schools were well-prepared to exploit the opportunities which it offered to improve their existing courses of study.

Paradoxically, this piecemeal recovery of classical knowledge was advantageous, for it forced logicians, mathematicians, theologians, and lawyers to confront the question of conflicting authorities and find a means of resolving the contradictions. As early as the ninth century, the Irishman John Scot Erigena, who knew Greek and grappled with the problems of human knowledge and the nature of God, proposed *ratio* – 'true reason' – as the means of distinguishing truth from error: 'Authority', he wrote, 'comes from true reason; true reason can never come from authority. Therefore, any authority which is not supported by true reason is inadequate.' So reason, supported by logic and mathematics, was exalted as the means of reducing the contradictions of traditional knowledge to harmony. The conflict between authorities produced a dynamic intellectual movement (discernible in canon law, Roman law, logic, theology and science), which enabled the Latin West to refashion its intellectual world.

The chief centres of this new learning were Paris and Laon for logic and theology, Bologna for Roman and canon law, Chartres and Orléans for rhetoric and poetry, Salerno and Toledo for access to Arab and Hebrew scholarship. Avid for the new knowledge, students from the whole of Christendom converged on these schools in very large numbers. 'In those days', wrote William the Breton, 'the study of letters flourished at Paris. We read that there was never in Athens or Egypt or any other place in the world such a multitude of scholars as those who dwelt at Paris for the sake of learning.'[1] Such large numbers forced the masters of Paris and the students at Bologna to organise themselves into associations – 'universities' – to protect their common interests and regulate the teaching and conferment of degrees, and so the university came into being as a corporate institution in the early years of the thirteenth century.

English scholars joined the throng of knowledge-hungry students in the continental schools. They also played a distinguished role in the rebirth and advancement of letters and learning in every field, and made a crucial contribution to the development of canon law and of science. In the vitally important work of translating texts from Arabic into Latin, for example, a line of distinguished successors carried on Adelard of Bath's pioneering work throughout the twelfth century. Robert of Chester translated Al-Khwarizmi's *Algebra* in Segovia in 1145, and wrote the earliest Latin treatise on the astrolabe, dated London 1147; Alfred the Englishman translated (*c.* 1200) the geological and alchemical parts of Avicenna's *Kitab al-Shifa*, and Michael the Scot (who became Frederick II's court astrologer) was

2.5. A page from an early English decretal collection

responsible for introducing to a Latin audience Averroes's commentaries on Aristotle's Metaphysics.[2]

John of Salisbury's account of his student days (1136–48) shows
that Englishmen were very prominent as teachers in Paris. Three of the
twelve masters whom he named were Englishmen: Robert Pullen,
Adam of the Little Bridge (du Petit Pont) and Robert of Melun (called
'of Melun' because he had made his reputation teaching in that city).[3]
By the end of the century, 16 of the 42 regent masters whose national
origins can be established were from England – which compares
favourably with the ten identifiable masters from the domains of the
French king. This achievement surpassed that of any other country or
region, and explains why, when the Arts Faculty of the University of
Paris organised itself into four nations *c.* 1215, the English Nation
dominated, and included all the Paris students from northern and
eastern Europe.[4]

When such scholars returned home, they brought with them not
only the fruits of their study, but also an international outlook, and
minds sharpened by logic or law. They played an important part in
the advancement of higher learning in the cathedral schools of Exeter,
London, Hereford and York, and in the establishment of universities
following the model of Paris, first at Oxford and later at Cambridge.
No other universities were founded north of the Alps, outside France,
until Charles IV founded the University of Prague in 1348, and most of
the other northern universities followed a century or more later. The
participation of English scholars in the essential work of translating
mathematical and astronomical works from Arabic led to the early
introduction of those works into the curriculum at Hereford and
Oxford, by teachers like Daniel of Morley (active *c.* 1170–90) and
Alexander Neckham (1157–1217). From these roots sprang the
distinctive school of experimental science at Oxford, founded by
Robert Grosseteste, bishop of Lincoln, and the university's first
chancellor. He investigated the physical properties of light and worked
on the mechanism of the human eye. He was the first Latin writer to
show how a prism breaks light into the colours of the spectrum and
his use of a lens to magnify small objects anticipated the invention of
spectacles by about 40 years. More importantly, he established the
crucial connection between theoretical speculation and experimental
verification upon which modern scientific method depends.[5]

English canonists contributed also to the development of ecclesiastical law. Medieval canon law was the common law of the Western
Church, binding on all members of Christian society from priest to
primate and from king to peasant. It defined the rights and duties of
clergy and religious as well as the general moral law for all Christians,
and it was enforced through ecclesiastical tribunals. Since knowledge

2.6. Pope Gregory IX
(from the Smithfield
Decretals)

of this law was essential to all ecclesiastical administrators, from archdeacons to bishops, canon law had by the 1120s taken its place beside the classical Roman law in Europe's major law school in Bologna, and by 1140–41 Master Gratian had completed a codification of the 'old' law of the church. English ecclesiastics were as anxious to learn the canon law as they were to learn Ovid or Euclid and Gratian's *Decretum* was being used in England within two decades of its composition. But the particular contribution of English canonists lay in their collection of papal replies to judicial appeals. These rescripts or *decretals* constituted the current law of the medieval church. Ultimately, the materials collected by English canon lawyers in

the twelfth century found their way into the *Decretals* promulgated by
Pope Gregory IX in 1234, and so became part of the permanent law of
the Western Church.[6]

The revival of learning also brought about a new flowering in
historical writing. Geoffrey of Monmouth's *History of the Britons*
gave literary expression to the traditions of the Welsh people and
made the Arthurian legends available to an educated audience; Gerald
of Wales's massive output is a mine of information about the state of
Wales and Ireland at the end of the twelfth century. For England,
monastic and clerical writing reached a standard never again equalled
in the middle ages. The monk William of Malmesbury, the regular

2.7. Artist's reconstruction of the exchequer at work

canon William of Newburgh, and secular priests like Roger of Howden, Ralph de Diceto, and William FitzStephen wrote chronicles and biographies of outstanding quality, equal to anything produced on the continent.[7]

Education was also a springboard for advance which enabled many English scholars to achieve brilliant success outside the schools. The most spectacular career of an Englishman abroad was that of Nicholas Breakspear, who became successively abbot of St Ruf, near Avignon (1137), cardinal bishop of Albano (1150), papal legate to Scandinavia (1152), and finally pope, with the title of Hadrian IV, in 1154 – the only Englishman ever to attain that honour. But there were many others. Robert Pullen (d. 1146), whom John of Salisbury heard lecture on theology in Paris, became the first English cardinal in 1143–4, and chancellor of the Roman church in 1144. His compatriot, Robert of Courson, rose to be cardinal (1202) and papal legate to France (1214–15), in which capacity he issued the first statutes for the University of Paris (1215). The career of John of Canterbury provides another outstanding example of the international influence of Englishmen at that time. A native of Canterbury, he was successively treasurer of York, bishop of Poitiers, and archbishop of Lyon, before retiring to the Cistercian monastery of Clairvaux. And from that retreat, he corresponded with Pope Innocent III on theological subjects including the doctrine of transubstantiation, more than ten years before its promulgation at the Fourth Lateran Council in 1215.[8]

But most English scholars returned home to influential positions in church and state. From the 1130s onwards, they formed a distinct professional élite, conscious of their status, and careful to record their educational achievement by retaining the title of *magister* – master – which they had acquired in the schools. We can trace the progressive entry of the *magistri* into the administration of bishopric and kingdom in the witness lists of contemporary charters. Nowhere is this more striking than in the household of the archbishops of Canterbury which, from the days of Theobald (1138–61), attracted a galaxy of educated talent. Herbert of Bosham recorded the distinction of Becket's household in his account of the *eruditi sancti Thome* (St Thomas's learned men).[9] Equally significant, the kings, from Henry I (1100–35) onwards, systematically recruited *magistri* to staff their expanding administration, so that by 1200 the English monarchy was far in advance of the French in its employment of 'schoolmen'.[10] The recently published *Biographical Dictionary of Scottish Graduates to A.D. 1410* – that is, of Scots who graduated before the foundation of Scotland's first University at St Andrews in 1410, and who must have received their degrees outside Scotland – tells the same story of the rapid introduction of university-trained clerks to office and influence in the Scottish kingdom.[11]

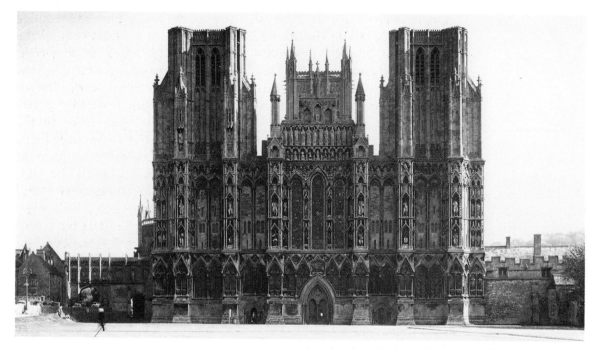

2.8. Wells Cathedral

This influx of trained men into public administration helped the establishment of stable bureaucratic institutions – the exchequer, the chancery, the judiciary – to support and implement royal government. Under Henry I, the exchequer (which had adopted the abacus, introduced into England by Robert of Lorraine) was organised as an efficient accounting office, with an annual audit of royal income drawn up each year at Michaelmas (29 September), and recorded on the Treasurer's Roll, called the Great Roll of the Pipe. The earliest surviving Pipe Roll (31 Henry I, for the year 1129–30) shows an already mature financial office in operation.[12] The series of Pipe Rolls survives almost complete from 1155 to 1819. Under Henry II, the foundations of the legal system were laid down in a series of Assizes (1166, 1176, 1181, 1184), with juries, perambulating justices and regularly-kept records of cases. By the end of the century, the English government was one of the most advanced and professional bureaucracies of the West, staffed by trained men, and producing three main categories of written public records: the Exchequer Rolls for finance, the Curia Regis Rolls, recording the judgements of the royal courts, and the Chancery Rolls, recording the charters and directives issued by the royal chancery. All this did much to rationalise, modernise and centralise royal government.

Traces of this medieval achievement in government, law and education survive to the present day in the departments of state, in the common law and the universities; but the most tangible and evocative survivals of the renaissance are to be found in architecture and the visual arts. Most of England's monasteries and cathedrals were built or rebuilt between 1080 and 1250. Unfortunately, two religious revolutions – the Reformation of the sixteenth century and the Puritan revolution of the seventeenth – between them destroyed the greater part of the religious art of the central middle ages. Some of the architecture which survived has been so restored and remodelled that its original quality is difficult to judge. The familiar west front of Westminster Abbey, for example, with its twin towers, is the later combined achievement of Sir Christopher Wren (who designed it) and Nicholas Hawksmoor (who supervised its construction); Salisbury's 'pure' Gothic owes as much to the work of James Wyatt at the end of the eighteenth century (1778–9) as to its medieval masons and architects, and Lichfield's facade and spires were 'restored' in the nineteenth century. And what has escaped the iconoclast and the restorer has often greatly suffered from the attacks of time and pollution. Nevertheless, enough has survived into the present day to demonstrate England's share in two major aesthetic movements – the Romanesque and the Gothic.

In Europe generally, apart from Italy, the twelfth century marked the transition from the monumental Romanesque style of architecture (exemplified by Cluny, Vézelay, Speyer, Maria Laach) to the soaring elegance of the Gothic, with its pointed arches, realistic sculpture, and stained glass (as at St Denis, Chartres, Sens, Amiens, Reims). English art experienced a comparable dramatic transformation in the wake of continental developments.

The introduction of the Romanesque style had begun with Edward the Confessor's refoundation of the monastery of St Peter at Westminster, but the assimilation of the style was accelerated by the Norman settlement. The new masters of church and state embarked on the construction of castles and the building or rebuilding of monasteries and cathedral churches on an unprecedented scale. William the Conqueror's White Tower, the cathedral churches of Durham and Winchester, the abbey churches of St Albans, Peterborough and Ely are impressive monuments to their achievement.

Meanwhile, the first fully Gothic edifice was realised with the completion of the monastic church of St Denis, then outside Paris, consecrated by Abbot Suger in 1144. And the style was brought into England in 1174 when Master William of Sens began work on 'Becket's crown', the magnificent new Choir and Trinity Chapel (into which the remains of Becket were later translated in 1220). But the style was quickly assimilated. An English Master William completed the work at Canterbury, when the Sens master was injured in a fall

2.9. The Prior's door,
Ely

2.10. Lincoln Cathedral

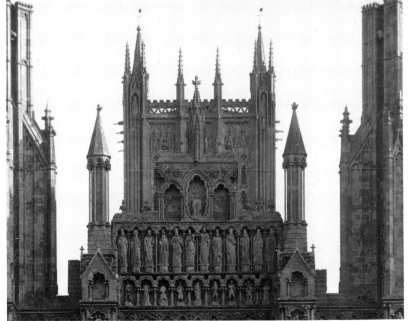

2.11. Wells Cathedral:
detail of carvings

from the scaffolding in 1179. Once received, the new style swept through England: work began on Wells to the design of Adam Lock in 1185; Lincoln followed from 1192, then Salisbury from 1219, and the new east end of Westminster Abbey from 1245. Although individual features were copied from French churches (Canterbury from Sens, Westminster from Reims and Amiens), English Gothic developed its own individuality, ranging from the 'tranquil and serene' Salisbury, designed by Nicholas of Ely, to the 'energy and activity' of Lincoln.[13] And the stained glass at Canterbury and York bear comparison with the great windows at Chartres and Reims.

From the beginning of the twelfth century, there is evidence of a revival in English sculpture. The Prior's door at Ely shows the work of an English craftsman, combining Viking and Anglo-Saxon motifs in a highly complex and intricate manner. The same imaginative combination is found at Peterborough and in the Romanesque fragments preserved in the facade at Lincoln, as well as in the finely-carved doorways of parish churches, such as Iffley in Oxfordshire and Kilpeck in Herefordshire. The Lewis chess set and the fragment of an ivory chair (both now in the British Museum) show the same taste. By the early thirteenth century, English sculptors were exploiting the greater opportunities which Gothic architecture afforded. The massive and imposing west front at Wells presents a vast stone screen once filled with crowned kings, sacred scenes and clergy robed for Mass. Though their colour has almost disappeared and their stone has been much eaten away, there is in the best of the figures a classical quality reminiscent of those on the west front of the cathedral in Reims. An even more evident classicism is found in the figure of St John, one of several statues surviving from the doorway of St Mary's Abbey in York (now in the Yorkshire Museum in York), and in the incomplete but very fine sculpture discovered in Winchester, portraying one of the Virtues or the Church. It is possible that the Winchester statue was copied from a Roman original brought back to England (in the mid-twelfth century) by Bishop Henry of Winchester, whose passion for collecting classical art was remarked on by John of Salisbury.[14]

Two of the most important monuments of English manuscript illumination in the period likewise resulted from Bishop Henry's patronage: the Winchester Psalter and the Winchester Bible. The former includes a remarkable instance of the cross-currents of cultural influence in English art at that time, in its depiction of the death of the Virgin, which so closely resembles a corresponding mosaic in a church in Palermo that the 'Winchester' illuminator must have seen either the original or a close derivative from it, though the rigour of the Sicilian mosaic has been somewhat softened in the English manuscript.[15] Although most churches would doubtless have been richly furnished

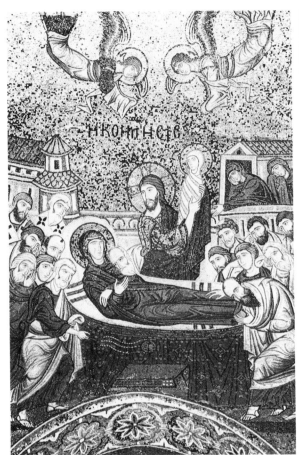

2.12a. Mosaic at Palermo showing the death of the Virgin
2.12b. Illustration of the death of the Virgin from the Winchester Psalter

with painted decoration, only tantalising fragments of wall-paintings survive from this period. Yet they reveal a comparable combination of English and continental traditions. Thus the remarkable wall-painting fragment from the St Anselm chapel in Canterbury, depicting St Paul on the island of Malta, demonstrates the fusion of English graphical skills with the iconographical traditions ultimately traceable to Byzantium.[16]

Why did this medieval renaissance come to an end? Like most questions about the causes of things, this has more than one possible answer. Perhaps the renaissance was almost too successful. Beginning in the late eleventh century as a challenge to customary ways of thought, and characterised in its early years by a creative drive to restore and reform the whole fabric of Christian society, the renaissance brought a new world into being. Christendom recovered the greater part of its classical and Christian heritage, and achieved profound intellectual and cultural advances on a very broad front. A new age of art, law, science and spirituality was created. But, just as the new Gothic art had become commonplace and stereotyped by the end of the thirteenth century so, despite its immense achievements, the new learning lost something of its creative originality and its power to challenge. Intellectually, the Christian West accommodated Aristotle – and with Thomas Aquinas assimilated his metaphysics into orthodox Christianity – just as it had earlier accommodated Plato. In many ways, the new order of the early twelfth century became the old order by the end of the thirteenth. Moreover, political, cultural and economic developments undermined the unity and confidence of Latin Christendom. Growing national consciousness and increasing tension and conflict between nations broke the West into hostile camps; the rise of vernacular languages (French, German, Italian, Castilian, Catalan) weakened the monopoly of Latin; and calamity followed economic calamity until the great plague of 1348–9 killed one third of the European population.

On the other hand, the twelfth century revival of European culture, learning and civilisation was not an isolated movement but the beginning of a process of dynamic evolution which culminated in the more famous renaissance of the fifteenth century. By enthroning reason and logic as the arbiters of truth, the leaders of the medieval enlightenment had established a criterion whereby each succeeding generation could examine and amend the wisdom inherited from its fathers, advancing the process of continuous renewal and change which distinguished western culture from the more static civilisations of India and China.

Further Reading

R.L. Benson and G. Constable (eds), *Renaissance and Renewal in the Twelfth Century* (Cambridge, Mass., 1982); C.N.L. Brooke, *The Twelfth Century Renaissance* (London, 1969); A.C. Crombie, *Robert Grosseteste and the Origins of Experimental Science 1100–1700* (Oxford, 1953); Joan Evans (ed.), *The Flowering of the Middle Ages* (London, 1966); C.H. Haskins, *The Renaissance of the Twelfth Century* (Cambridge, Mass., 1927); Margaret Rickert, *Painting in Britain: The Middle Ages* (London, 1954); R.W. Southern, 'The Place of England in the Twelfth Century Renaissance', *History*, XLV (1960), pp. 201–16, revised in *Medieval Humanism and Other Studies* (Oxford, 1970).

CHAPTER THREE

Magna Carta and Royal Government

John Gillingham

In 1215 a powerful group of English barons rose in rebellion against King John and, at Runnymede, forced him to set his seal to Magna Carta – the most famous document in English history.[1] This sequence of events is well-known, so familiar indeed that we are inclined to take it for granted. This means that we are in danger of forgetting that in reality it was all very surprising.

Not that there was anything surprising about a baronial revolt. There had been rebellions against William I, William II, Henry I, Stephen, Henry II, and Richard – in other words against every king since the Norman Conquest. What was surprising was the fact that the rebellion against John led to the drawing up of a document, a detailed programme of governmental reform. This was an unprecedented action, a revolutionary step forward – though since the rebels looked to the past for their definition of a 'golden age' in the relationship between king and subjects it might be better described as a revolutionary step backward. When John lost London to the rebels and decided that he had to bow, at any rate temporarily, to their demands, he was in effect accepting the existence of a written constitution, the first written constitution in European history.[2] Since then, of course, Englishmen have come to pride themselves on precisely their unwritten constitution, so there is something of a paradox here as well.

There is indeed much that is paradoxical in the history of Magna Carta. The charter itself could be accurately described as a 'highly successful total failure'. It was successful in that it became the first

3.1. Detail of Magna Carta

statute of the realm. When later generations of lawyers compiled their books of statutes it was always Magna Carta which had pride of place. The whole thing more or less intact remained on the Statute Book until the Law Reform Act of 1863 and a dozen of its provisions survived until well into the present century. But it was not just in England that it came to enjoy the status of a fundamental law. Taken to the American colonies in the seventeenth century it influenced both the laws of individual states and the Constitution of the United States. 'Nor shall any persons be deprived of life, liberty or property, without due process of law.' The resounding phrases of the Fifth Amendment are an obvious echo of Magna Carta Chapter 39. Over the centuries Magna Carta became what it is today, a potent symbol of men's struggle for freedom and human rights. Thus it was only natural that those who saw John F. Kennedy as a champion of liberty should choose Runnymede as the site for his memorial. In the recent Commons debate on trade unions at GCHQ, Magna Carta was more than once invoked, much as it was quoted by seventeenth century lawyers, men like Coke and Selden, in their defence of liberties of the subject against the tyrannical powers of the crown. No other medieval law remotely approaches Magna Carta in its fame and lasting relevance.[3]

Yet in 1215 Magna Carta was an abysmal failure. It was meant to be a peace treaty, a formula which would put an end to the conflict between king and barons. In fact civil war broke out again within three months of the meeting at Runnymede. Its failure in the short run is quite as striking as its success in the long term. By looking at the

3.2. Victorian representation of John setting his seal to Magna Carta

events leading up to and surrounding Magna Carta, we can see medieval kingship at a moment of crisis. This can help us to understand what kingship involved and how medieval government operated. For this was a form of government in which the king himself was the single most important component. To appreciate this fully we must try to answer three major questions. First, why did the rebels of 1215 decide to take the novel step of drawing up a reform programme? Secondly, why did Magna Carta fail to achieve its immediate purpose of bringing peace? And thirdly, how was it that this failed treaty came to be looked upon as 'the cornerstone of English liberties'?

We begin with rebellion since Magna Carta was, above all else, the product of rebellion. In order to understand why rebellions occurred as often as they did we must look at some of the basic features of the medieval political system. Fundamental was the fact that a great deal of the country's landed wealth was concentrated in the hands of a small but immensely powerful élite – the royal dynasty and a few dozen baronial families. This meant that political stability depended on the state of relationships within the élite. This in turn meant that the king's primary function was a managerial one; his job was to ensure that these relationships remained reasonably harmonious.

How did he do this? To answer this question we must bear in mind that the barons were also the king's tenants – in legal jargon they were his tenants-in-chief. They held their estates from the king. In return they were expected to serve and aid the king: essentially this meant political service and, in times of war, military service and financial aid. In addition, a tenant-in-chief's heir had to pay a duty, known as a relief, in order to enter into his inheritance, while if he – or she – were under age, then the king took the estates into his custody, to do with them very much as he pleased (subject to certain conventions). In these circumstances the king controlled his ward's marriage. If there were no direct heirs then, after provision had been made for the widow – where re-marriage was also subject to crown control – the king could grant the land out again to whomever he pleased. This degree of control over the inheritances and marriages of the wealthiest people in the realm meant that the king's powers of patronage were immense.[4] He had at his disposal not only offices; he had heirs, heiresses and widows. Thus when Richard I gave to William Marshall the heiress to the earldom of Pembroke he, in effect, made William a millionaire overnight. No head of government in the western world of today has anything remotely approaching the power of patronage in the hands of a medieval English king. This is why the royal court was the focal point of the whole political system, a turbulent, lively factious place in which men – and a few women – pushed and jostled each other in desperate attempts to catch the king's eye. Not surprisingly it was a medieval literary convention to describe a courtier's life as sheer hell.[5] But standing at the mouth of hell there were hundreds who were only too keen to enter.

The problem was that, in the nature of things, there were never enough posts, heirs, heiresses and widows to go round. For every William Marshall who had reason to be satisfied with his share of royal patronage, there were bound to be several who were disappointed. Every act of royal generosity thwarted other people's expectations. Thus there was always bound to be a group of disgruntled and discontented men. These men were not trying to overturn the system. They were merely trying to obtain what they believed to be their fair share of royal patronage. Whether a king was reputedly strong like Henry I or weak like Stephen, these men, given half a chance, would rebel. Rebellion, in other words, was an established part of the structure of medieval politics.

But if the very nature of the political system explains, in a general way, why rebellions were always a possibility to be reckoned with, it still remains to explain why it was that this particular revolt, the Magna Carta revolt, occurred.[6] For this there are a multitude of reasons but two stand out as being particularly important. In the first place John's handling of patronage was peculiarly ham-fisted. It was standard practice for kings to use the patronage system as a handy source of income. Men offered money in order to obtain what the king had to offer: offices, succession to estates, custody of land, wardship and marriage. All these were to be had at a price and the price was negotiable. At times there might be quite a lively auction, and although the king, of course, was under no compulsion to accept the highest bid, here was an area where he could, if he chose, raise more money by consistently driving harder bargains. John drove some very hard bargains indeed. A northern baron, Nicholas de Stuteville, offered 10,000 marks (£6,666) for the succession to his brother's estates. Just how stiff a price this was can be seen from the fact that Magna Carta was to fix the proper rate for the relief to a barony at the very much lower sum of £100. It comes as no surprise to find Nicholas de Stuteville among the rebels of 1215.

Clearly patronage could be used as a way of soaking the rich, but it could also be manipulated as an instrument of political discipline. Early in John's reign, for example, William de Broase bid 5,000 marks (£3,333) for the lordship of Limerick in Ireland. William was one of the king's closest associates and the exchequer made little or no effort to collect the debt. It was often thus, and the expectation that the exchequer would not press too hard had the effect of making ambitious men offer more than they could afford. But in 1208 William de Broase fell out of favour and at once the exchequer came knocking at his door. In the end William was driven into exile while his wife and eldest son died in one of John's prisons. It was a system which tempted men to speculate and then hit them hard when they were in trouble. From John's point of view it offered a splendid mechanism for forcing men to be loyal. With the fate of William de Broase before his eyes a baron who was in the king's debt would think twice before stepping out of line.

What those who were in debt thought about it is, of course, quite another matter. Take, for example, the extraordinarily revealing case of John de Lacy, constable of Chester and lord of Pontefract. In 1213 he succeeded to his father's estates, but only after agreeing to pay 7,000 marks (£4,666). He was given three years to pay, and encouraged by the prospect of having the debt reduced by 1,000 marks if, in the meantime, he gave loyal service. This he did. In 1214 he went on campaign with John when many barons would not join the king. In March 1215 he was one of the few barons to swear to go on crusade with John. By now John was facing considerable difficulties and he was correspondingly appreciative of de Lacy's loyalty. The day after de Lacy took the cross he was pardoned all his debts. At last he had some freedom of action. Two months later he

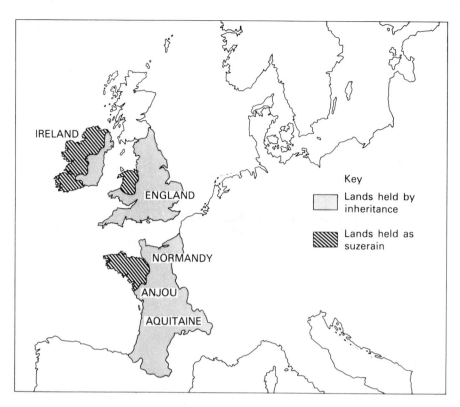

3.3a. The Angevin Empire in 1200

Key

Lands held by inheritance

Lands held as suzerain

joined the rebels. The Magna Carta movement, it has been well said, was 'a rebellion of the King's debtors'[7] – but even those who had escaped from the toils of indebtedness resented the way in which John had reduced the time-honoured values of good lordship and faithful service to nothing more than a calculation of profit and loss. John's trouble was that he lacked the happy knack of inspiring loyalty. So, he exploited one of the strongest cards in the king's hand – his power of patronage – in an attempt to compel men to be loyal. For a while it seemed to work, but in the end he over-played his hand.

The second reason for the rebellion against John was that by 1215 he was a thoroughly discredited king.[8] He had come to the throne in 1199 as the ruler of the most powerful state in Europe. For nearly two hundred years England had been just one country within a wider empire: first a part of Cnut's North Sea empire (1016–35); 1040–42); then a part of the Norman cross-channel empire (1066–1144); finally from 1154 onwards part of the Angevin Empire which had been cobbled together as a result of Henry Plantagenet's thrusting ambition. Like his father Henry II and his brother Richard Coeur de Lion, John was not just king of England. Thus the opening words of Magna Carta: 'John, by the grace of God, King of England, Lord of Ireland, Duke of Normandy and Aquitaine, Count of Anjou. . . .' As

3.3b. The Angevin
Empire in 1204

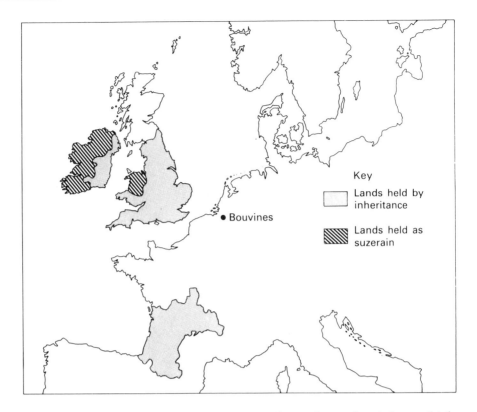

this list of titles makes plain, John had inherited vast dominions which
stretched from Ireland and the Scottish border in the north to Gascony
and the Pyrenees in the south.[9] In 1199 there was no one in Europe
who could match the resources at John's disposal. Yet by 1215 he had
been outmanoeuvred and defeated time and again.

In two disastrous years, 1203 and 1204, he contrived to lose
Normandy, Anjou and much of Poitou. His maladroit handling of the
powerful Lusignan family had provoked a rebellion in Poitou; his
murder of his own nephew, Arthur of Brittany, had led to him being
regarded with mingled distrust and distaste. In striking contrast to his
brother and predecessor Richard, he had been unable to retain the
confidence of the most powerful princes of France; in consequence
when the king of France, Philip Augustus, launched his armies against
Normandy and Anjou, John found himself isolated and incapable of
organising adequate defences.[10]

In the history of English kingship the events of 1203–4 constituted
an important turning point. Since 1066 England had been ruled by
Frenchmen: first Normans and then the Plantagenets of Anjou. It is
thus not surprising to find that some modern English historians have,
in effect, breathed a sigh of patriotic relief when discussing the loss of
Normandy and Anjou. Now at last the Plantagenets were free to

3.4. The seal of King John

become true English rulers. They could shake off the incubus of the continent, stay 'at home' and look after their 'real' subjects. But this is not how it was. The loss of Normandy and Anjou did not mean that an English king had lost two outlying provinces. It meant that the heart had been torn out of the Angevin Empire. John became an English king only by default and against his will. From now on he was known by the contemptuous nickname of 'Softsword'. As one troubadour put it:

> No one may ever trust him
> For his heart is soft and cowardly.[11]

John knew that to retrieve his reputation he would one day have to recover Normandy and Anjou.

He spent almost ten years preparing his counter-strike against Philip Augustus. He built up a coalition of allies and adopted a strategy intended to force the Capetian king to divide his forces. This was the policy which had worked well in Richard's reign. Unfortunately for John he lacked his brother's supreme competence in the field of war. The decisive battle of Bouvines (27 July 1214) ended in an overwhelming victory for Philip Augustus; and that defeat sealed John's fate as surely as defeat in the Falklands sealed the fate of General Gualtieri. As soon as John heard the news of Bouvines he began to prepare for civil war in England.

So in one sense the rebellion of 1215 was anything but surprising. A regime which was both arbitrary and tarred with the brush of humiliating military failure was surely a doomed regime. But would-be rebels had their problems too. They needed a cause. If they were to win widespread support, they could not afford to be seen as men fighting for their own private interests. Yet, as we have seen, the rebels of 1215 were precisely that. They were the excluded, the disappointed; men who had done badly in the fierce competition for the king's favour. So too, of course, were most rebels, but the rebels of 1215 had to cope with a problem which their predecessors had not had to face. Hitherto rebels had been able to present themselves as men fighting for the legitimate rights of a disinherited member of the royal family: for Robert of Normandy against his brothers, William Rufus and Henry I: for Matilda against Stephen; for Henry II's adolescent sons

3.5. Henry II (top left), Richard I (top right), John (bottom left), Henry III (bottom right)

against their father; for John against Richard. But in John's reign the accidents of birth and death – accidents which were pushed in the right direction when John had his nephew Arthur murdered – meant that there were no royal princes whose discontents could serve as a focus for revolt. John's own sons were still much too young. The only possible claimant was Prince Louis of France but he was only distantly related – he was husband of one of Henry II's grand-daughters – and after the wars of the last generation the son of King Philip Augustus was unlikely to have made a popular anti-king. In this awkward predicament, John's opponents took their step into the unknown. Lacking a prince they devised a document. They invented a new kind of focus for revolt, a programme of reform, a charter of liberties. If they could not fight for the rights of a prince, then they would fight instead for the rights of the whole realm, for the community of the whole land.

In doing this, the rebels of 1215 were following a path marked out, not by former rebels, but by kings. Kings had of course granted charters before. They had granted charters to individuals and to communities – ecclesiastical communities and urban communities. Then there were the communities of the shire. From the 1190s onward first Richard and then John began to grant rights and privileges to shire communities. From here it was a natural progression to conceive of the whole realm as a community, a corporate body capable of possessing rights and liberties. More than a century earlier indeed, in the year 1100, King Henry I had granted a charter 'to all his barons and faithful men'.[12] By the winter of 1214 John's opponents had, as it were, resurrected this charter and were using it as a frame around which they could formulate their own demands. They were helped in this by the fact that some of the grievances which were uppermost in their minds had also been dealt with in Henry I's charter – abuses of royal patronage in particular. But important though this charter was as a model for Magna Carta there were several crucial differences. Henry's charter had been a sort of election manifesto issued on the occasion of his coronation in August 1100. Like most election manifestos it promptly became a dead letter once he was sitting firmly on the throne and not until John's reign did its ghost rise up to haunt a later king. By contrast the genesis of Magna Carta made it much more memorable. It had been forced out by rebellion. It was given maximum publicity. And right from the start it was intended to last; it was a charter granted 'to all the free men of the realm and their heirs for ever'.

Thus, despite the existence of these earlier charters, the fact remains that never before had there been anything quite like Magna Carta. As the product of rebellion it was conceived and drawn up in an

atmosphere of crisis. Both John and his enemies were appealing for political and military support. In these circumstances the barons could not afford to be identified with a programme which suited only their own sectional interests. They ended up with a charter of liberties which was long, detailed and contained something for everyone. Thus Magna Carta took shape not just as a criticism of the way John had been treating the barons, but as a thoroughgoing commentary on the whole system of royal government.

Why then did Magna Carta fail in 1215? The fact is that it was bound to fail. Given the system within which they worked the barons had created a political monstrosity, one which could not possibly be expected to survive for long. Naturally no king can be expected to look kindly on a document which has been extorted from him by force of arms. No one would expect him to implement its terms with enthusiasm. But the problem with Magna Carta went deeper than this. The rebels had foreseen John's reluctance. They had anticipated that he would try to wriggle out of the commitments made at Runnymede and they had set up machinery designed to meet this eventuality. Chapter 52 of Magna Carta reads as follows:

> If, without lawful judgement of his peers, we have deprived anyone of lands, castles, liberties or rights, we will restore them to him at once. And if any disagreement arises on this let it be settled by the judgement of the 25 barons. . . .

Who were these 25 barons? Chapter 61 tells us:

> the barons shall choose any 25 barons of the realm they wish . . . so that if we or any of our servants offend in any way . . . then those 25 barons together with the community of the whole land shall distrain and distress us in every way they can, namely by seizing castles, lands and possessions . . . until in their judgement amends have been made.

Clearly if, in the last resort, everything was to depend upon the judgement of the 25 and if, further, the 25 were empowered to seize the king's castles, lands and possessions whenever they thought it necessary, then the king had in effect been dethroned. This was not merely to reform the realm; this was to destroy the sovereignty of the crown.

No medieval king could have submitted to Magna Carta except, as John did in June 1215, as a tactical manoeuvre designed to gain time and put his enemies off their guard. So deep was the distrust between them that it is unlikely that any agreement could have preserved the peace for long. But a peace treaty which included Chapters 52 and 61 made it certain that the renewed outbreak of war would come sooner rather than later. In this sense Magna Carta was the cause of its own undoing. By mid-July, at the very latest, John had written to the pope asking him to annul the charter. By the autumn the rebels had realised that the king had no intention of keeping his promises. They sent a request for help to the court of France. They offered the throne to Prince Louis, and he accepted. This was a reversion to the old style of rebellion. Once again rebels were taking up arms on behalf of a rival king. By offering the crown to Louis the barons were publicly acknowledging the fact that the new style had failed. Denounced by the king, discarded by the rebels, Magna Carta was surely dead.

Yet it survived. And here we come to the third of our questions and to yet another of the paradoxes of Magna Carta. A failure when used by rebels as a weapon against the crown, it succeeded when it was taken over by royalists and turned against the rebels. How are we to explain this ironic twist of fortune? John died in October 1216 leaving as his heir a nine-year-old boy, the young Henry III, and a kingdom torn in two by civil war. Within a month of the child's coronation his advisers had re-issued Magna Carta, shorn, of course, of its more objectionable chapters. By doing this Henry III's counsellors intended to cut the ground from beneath the feet of the barons who had called in Louis of France. In that sense, re-issuing Magna Carta was a propaganda move – and probably an effective one. But it was not merely that. Minor changes in the text of some of its clauses show that the detail of the document was being studied carefully and thoughtfully. For example, the charter of 1215 promised that an heir

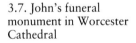
3.7. John's funeral monument in Worcester Cathedral

who had been in wardship should have his inheritance when he came of age without having to pay a relief. The charter of 1216 made the same promise and then went on to fix the age at which an heir reached his majority, 'namely when he is 21 years old'. Magna Carta was clearly regarded as a serious statement of the law of the land, worth modifying, worth keeping up-to-date, not just as a propaganda document to be jettisoned as soon as the emergency had passed.

When Louis of France conceded defeat, after two years of civil war, in the autumn of 1217, Magna Carta was reissued again, and with further modifications. These included the issue of a supplementary charter dealing with forest law. Since the Forest Charter was a much smaller document, the main charter became known as the 'big charter', Magna Carta. In 1225 the charter was reissued yet again, this time in return for a grant of taxation to the king. The text of 1225 is important because it was this version (and not the Runnymede one) which entered the Statute Books and so became the Magna Carta of subsequent history. These frequent reissues helped to keep the charter before men's eyes. Moreover, like the original charter of 1215, the reissues were read out at meetings of the county courts, translated into French or English, or both. (Presumably if it had been read out in Latin, people would have either rioted or fallen asleep.) All this meant that the charter quickly became both very well known and generally regarded as 'a good thing', a touchstone of good government. Believing it to be 'a good thing' men came to believe that it contained what they wanted it to contain. In this way, the charter very quickly took on a mythical life of its own.

From now on whenever a king was felt to be governing badly, to be infringing men's liberties, then the cry went up for the confirmation of the charters. From now on whenever opponents of the crown put forward reform programmes of their own – notably the Provisions of 1258 and 1259, the Ordinances of 1311, and later the Petition of Right in 1628 and the Grand Remonstrance in 1641 – they believed that they were following in the footsteps of the men who had made Magna Carta. As a venerable symbol of the fight against tyranny it still has its value today.

Further Reading

M.T. Clanchy, *England and its Rulers, 1066–1272* (London, 1983); J. Gillingham, *The Angevin Empire* (London, 1984); J.C. Holt, *Magna Carta* (Cambridge, 1965); A. Pallister, *Magna Carta: The Heritage of Liberty* (Oxford, 1971); R.W. Southern, *Medieval Humanism and other Studies* (Oxford, 1970); W.L. Warren, *King John* (London, 1961).

CHAPTER FOUR

War, Politics and Parliament

Chris Given-Wilson

English people rather like to talk about their parliament at Westminster as the 'mother of parliaments'; by which they mean not only that it was a prototype for other democratic institutions in different parts of the world, but also that it has a very long history. In fact the history of the English parliament goes back to the thirteenth century. On the other hand, it is not quite as typical as we might think. What makes the English parliament rather different from other similar bodies elsewhere is the fact that under the English system it is the lower house, the House of Commons, which has the real power, not the upper house, the House of Lords. What needs to be explained therefore, is not simply how parliament came into being, but also how and why it was that the commons came to play such an important role in parliament.

There is no doubt that, even as early as the middle of the fourteenth century, everyone realised that not only parliament, but the commons as a vital part of parliament, were here to stay. But parliaments then were very different affairs from modern parliaments. Nowadays, parliaments last four or five years; in the middle ages, they lasted a few weeks. Nowadays we have universal franchise; in the middle ages, only the wealthy could vote. Even in the last hundred and fifty years or so, parliament has seen tremendous changes; the Reform Bills of the nineteenth century, which enfranchised the male population, for example, or the suffragette movement, which fought to win the vote for women. So the history of parliament is a history of constant evolution. And if we go back to the beginning, and search for the origins of that evolutionary process, we find what is perhaps a slightly unexpected starting-point in warfare.

Politics in late medieval England was dominated by warfare. From the late thirteenth century until the middle of the fifteenth century,

4.1a. A medieval battle scene

4.1b. Detail showing a medieval knight

England was almost constantly in a state of war with France, or Scotland, or quite frequently both.[1] This was the age of the Hundred Years War (the traditional dates of which are 1337–1453, but which in reality formed only part of an Anglo-French struggle lasting from the 1290s until the end of the middle ages). Success in war was vital to a medieval king. Consider, for example, the fate of those English kings who failed in war. Edward II led an English army into what was probably the most humiliating defeat of the whole middle ages, when the Scottish king, Robert Bruce, crushed his army at Bannockburn in 1314; ten years later he stumbled into another unsuccessful war, this time with the French, and in 1327 he was deposed. Richard II, on the other hand, showed little inclination to fight the French at all, and it is abundantly clear that many of his nobles thought that he should.[2] He, too, was deposed, in 1399. And then there was Henry VI. It was during Henry's reign, in 1453 to be precise, that the English were

4.2. The battle of Agincourt

finally expelled from the lands which they had held in France since the twelfth century, and in 1461 Henry was deposed as well.[3]

Military failure was not the only reason why any of these kings was deposed; they were all thoroughly unsatisfactory rulers in many ways. But for kings, warfare was not just a hobby; it was their duty. There was a well-known literary convention in the middle ages, which classified society in three orders, or estates: those who pray (the clergy), those who work (the peasants), and those who fight (the nobility).[4] And among the nobility, the greatest was the king. To protect his people, therefore, and to pursue quarrels in a just cause was a solemn and God-ordained obligation imposed on a king. When we look at the prestige and the popularity enjoyed by those kings who *were* successful in war – Edward III, for instance, under whom the French army was destroyed at Crécy, and the Scots decisively defeated at Halidon Hill, or Henry V, whose dazzling victory at Agincourt made him a national hero – then it soon becomes clear that success abroad greatly eased the path of kingship at home.

So prestige was important; projecting the right image always is. But success in war also brought more tangible benefits: conquered

4.3. Henry V of England

territories, for example, which could be distributed as rewards to the king's followers. Henry V certainly recognised this. After his victory at Agincourt in 1415, he set out systematically to conquer Normandy, and having conquered Normandy, he proceeded to grant out a whole host of lands, titles and offices there to Englishmen. In making these grants, Henry was not only looking to the past, he was also looking to the future; as well as rewarding his followers, he was creating in these men a vested interest in England's continued rule of Normandy, and that, arguably, was the best way to maintain the conquest.[5]

The profits of war came in many different guises. Conquered territories apart, there was plunder, there was tribute, and there were ransoms.[6] Plunder was virtually institutionalised in medieval warfare; there was a convention, for example, that when a town was successfully besieged, the commander of the besieging army would allow his troops to loot the town for a given period, sometimes up to three days. At the same time, occupied territories would be forced to pay tribute without compunction, often on a systematic basis: it was protection money, in effect. There is no doubt that large parts of France suffered terribly from these ravages in the later middle ages; the problem for them, of course, being that the war was fought almost entirely on French soil.[7]

But in terms of money profits, Edward III far outstripped any other

4.4. Soldiers looting a house

medieval king. The reason why he did so is simple – ransoms. Edward III did what every English king must have dreamed of doing: he actually captured his two main rivals. In 1346, at the battle of Neville's Cross, just outside Durham, the Scottish king David Bruce was taken prisoner; ten years later at the battle of Poitiers, King John of France suffered a similar fate. In fact, Edward III himself was not actually present at either of these battles, but that did not matter. His commanders were acting in his name, and it was Edward who claimed the prisoners (with due compensation, naturally, to the captors). Both kings were sent to the Tower, and both were put to ransom.[8] David Bruce's ransom was, after lengthy negotiations, set at £100,000. But John of France, who is known as John the Good, or rather less flatteringly, as John the Mediocre, and who was after all king of a much larger and much richer country than Scotland, had to pay half a million pounds for his freedom. This was a staggering sum, about six or seven times the average yearly income of the English exchequer. As it turned out, not all of it was paid – but over half of it was, and for a time, Edward III was a fabulously rich king.

Windsor Castle is the chief monument to Edward's wealth. He was born at Windsor, and it was here that he invested his profits of war in

4.6. John 'the Mediocre' of France

4.7. Windsor Castle: St George's Chapel

the 1360s.[9] In the upper bailey of the castle, he built a new series of fortifications, and a splendid new range of royal apartments. In the lower bailey, he built a magnificent chapel to St George, to serve as the ceremonial centre for the Order of the Garter, which Edward had founded in the 1340s. Windsor, of course, has undergone several rebuildings since then. In the late fifteenth century, Edward IV built another, even more splendid, chapel of St George. Early in the nineteenth century, King George IV had the royal apartments completely refurbished. Even so, Windsor Castle as we see it today is still, essentially, very much the creation of Edward III, and it was largely the French king's ransom which paid for it. Ironically, King John himself spent several months imprisoned here.

Warfare, then, could be very profitable, not only in political terms, but also in financial terms. But that did not mean that the war could be made to pay for itself. Kings like Edward III and Henry V clearly regarded the profits which they made from war as personal profits, to be spent as they liked. In addition, there were long periods during which the war was not profitable at all – usually when it was going badly. So, as is almost invariably the case, prolonged warfare meant a continuous drain on the exchequer.

Moreover, warfare was becoming increasingly expensive in the later middle ages. There were several reasons for this: developments in armour, for example. Around 1300, a typical English knight's armour would have consisted of a chain-mail coat, called a hauberk, stretching from his shoulders down to his hips; a large cylindrical iron helmet for his head; and probably metal leggings to protect the lower part of his body. He rode on a great destrier (or warhorse), and carried a lance, a shield, a sword, and perhaps a battle-axe as well. A hundred years later, he would have been dressed very differently. By then the chain-mail hauberk had been discarded, and instead the knight would have been covered from head to toe in plate armour; on his head, instead of the heavy iron helmet, he would wear a much lighter bascinet, with a movable visor. The weapons he carried changed little but one advantage of the extra protection which he got from his plate armour was that he now carried a much smaller and more manoeuvrable shield. In fact, he might even dispense with the shield altogether.

But the disadvantage with plate armour was that it took a lot more skill to make than chain-mail – indeed it was often made individually – and that made it more expensive. For the infantrymen too, the rank and file of the army, equipment had become much more expensive; in Edward I's day, at the end of the thirteenth century, it cost about five shillings to equip an infantryman for war; by 1350, it cost nearer £2. Armies were more professional now, and higher standards were expected. Gunpowder too was being used more and more, and this pushed up costs in other ways; fortifications had to be strengthened. Town and castle walls had to be thickened; gun platforms were constructed around them. And the cannons themselves were not cheap. One, called Mons Meg, was probably made for the Scottish king James II in the middle of the fifteenth century. It weighs over five tons, and could fire cannon-balls weighing about 300 lb. But new technology, as well as being expensive, could also be dangerous: James himself was killed during the siege of Roxburgh in 1460, when one of his own cannons exploded on firing and he was hit by shrapnel.

This development in military hardware was not the only reason for the rising cost of war. From the king's point of view, there was another, fundamental, reason. The way in which armies were raised was changing.[10] Traditionally, the early fourteenth century marks the changeover from so-called 'feudal armies' to what are known as 'contract armies'. Instead of summoning men to fight for him because they were his vassals – in other words, because they held land from him in feudal tenure – the king would now make contracts (called indentures) with men to fight for him in return for wages. In fact, this changeover was not as sudden as it might appear. It is very doubtful whether any English royal army, throughout the middle ages, was raised purely on the basis of a feudal summons. When William the Conqueror invaded England in 1066, he brought numerous mercen-

4.8. Mons Meg

aries with him as well as his Norman vassals. Moreover, it became increasingly common for kings to commute the military service which their vassals owed to them: in other words, the king demanded a payment (called scutage) in lieu of service and then used the money to hire mercenaries or pay retainers. However, feudal summonses did continue to play an important part in the raising of royal armies right through the twelfth and thirteenth centuries. Even in Edward I's reign, several of the king's armies were essentially feudal. Yet within twenty years of Edward's death, the feudal element in English armies was almost obsolete. By 1330, at the latest, *everyone* who fought in the English king's army was being paid for his service. And this, even more than the improvements in equipment, made it more and more difficult for the king to find enough money to finance his wars.

So what could the king do to meet these escalating costs? A medieval king had two main sources of income; first, his profits from land and lordship – what might be termed his traditional revenues; and secondly, taxation.[11] In theory, a feudal king had no right to impose general taxation on his people. He could, in certain circumstances, ask for payments from the men who held land from him (these were called aids) but that was not at all the same as general taxation. By the thirteenth century, however, two facts were becoming painfully clear. The first was that the king's traditional revenues – his profits from land and lordship – were quite simply failing to provide him with enough money, especially if he was fighting a war. The second was that the wealth of the country was becoming much more diversified: the growth of towns and markets, the development of trade and commerce – things which were happening not just in England, of course, but all over western Europe – made it absolutely imperative for the king to find ways of tapping this new wealth. In other words, he needed to establish his right to tax *all* his subjects, and since in theory he had no right to take taxes, he had no option but to obtain consent for them.

This is where parliament comes into the picture. In order to win consent for general taxation, the king had to prove that he needed the money. So gradually a compromise evolved: the king's requests for taxation would be based on a plea of national emergency, and in practice this almost invariably meant a military emergency. It might be defensive, the threat of foreign invasion, for example; or it might be offensive, such as the need to send an army abroad. Thus, the king claimed it was in the national interest, to deal with a threat to the nation, that a tax should be granted; public money must be raised to be spent in the public interest. As long as he could convince his subjects that his need was genuine, and as long as he went about obtaining consent in the proper way, he would usually get his tax.

But what *was* the proper way to obtain consent? At first, kings tried to get consent for taxation in a variety of ways: from merchants, from townsmen, or from groups of barons meeting in council. But gradually, the range of options narrowed. The consenting assemblies became more systematic and, as they did so, it became more and more common to describe them as parliaments. It was at the end of the thirteenth century, with the new round of hostilities against France and Scotland in particular, that the pressure of war, and the king's demands for taxation, really began to escalate. And, from this time onwards, it was more or less accepted that parliament was the place where he obtained consent for his taxation.

So the link between warfare and parliament is a direct one: it was in order to finance warfare that taxation was granted, and it was largely in order to get consent for taxation that parliaments were summoned. But the equation is not quite as simple as that. We first begin to find the word 'parliament' used in England in the 1240s, and what it really means at this time is an extended meeting of the king's council.[12] Now this raises a problem: if parliaments were already meeting in the mid-thirteenth century, and yet it was only in the *late* thirteenth century that they began to grant taxes on a regular basis, then just how important was the question of taxation in giving birth to parliament? Well the answer, I think, is that if we go right back to the very beginnings of parliament, taxation did not play an important part at all. The word 'parliament' comes from the French verb *parler* – to talk. The earliest parliaments were essentially discussion meetings, or talking-shops. They provided an opportunity for the king to gather information, to issue ordinances, to dispense justice. Henry III, who reigned from 1216 to 1272, held about seventeen parliaments, and they were very haphazard affairs indeed. Their composition varied enormously, their functions were ill-defined, they had no rules for procedure. In the thirteenth century we should not talk of 'parliament', in the singular, as an institution, but of 'parliaments', in the plural, as occasions.

But why taxation was so important in the origins of parliament was because it gave shape, and permanence, and ultimately, power to these haphazard gatherings. By the middle of the fourteenth century it was accepted – indeed it was laid down by statute – that only parliaments (in practice, the commons in parliament) could grant the king taxation. By this time the composition of parliament was also well-established, and there were clear procedural guidelines. In a word, parliament had become an institution.

So what was a parliament at this time? And who were the commons? During the fourteenth century, parliaments met on average about once a year, usually at Westminster. At a full session, about three hundred and fifty people would be present, and they can be divided into two main groups. First came the lords, of whom there were about a hundred, ranging from bishops and abbots to dukes, earls, and other great landholders. All the lords were summoned individually – that was what distinguished them from the commons.[13] Secondly, there were the commons. They numbered about two hundred and thirty, made up of two knights from each shire, and two burgesses from each of the larger towns, or boroughs. They were not summoned individually, but elected in the shire or borough courts. So already, as early as the fourteenth century, the structure of parliament foreshadows the later division into two houses, Lords and Commons.

Although they were numerically superior to the lords, it would be wrong to exaggerate the power of the commons in medieval parliaments. In the great majority of parliaments, right through the middle ages, it was the lords who dominated meetings. Yet there clearly were occasions when it was the commons who took the initiative: take for example the so-called 'Good Parliament' of 1376, probably the most famous parliament of the middle ages.[14]

The Good Parliament met at a very difficult time: the war with

4.9. The Palace of Westminster before the fire of 1834

France was going badly, the level of taxation was high, and worst of all, the country was virtually leaderless. Edward III was senile and had lost his grip on government; his eldest son the Black Prince was dying – he died, in fact, during the session. Parliament met on 28 April. As usual, the proceedings began with a speech from the chancellor, and then the members split into two groups: the lords met in the White Chamber of Westminster Palace (the old palace, that is, which was largely burnt down in 1834), while the commons went to the chapter house at Westminster Abbey. Clearly, the commons were in an angry mood from the start. They began to talk among themselves, making accusations against the king's ministers, setting out a programme of reform. They swore to be loyal to one another, and took an oath to keep their discussions secret. Eventually, they chose a spokesman to represent them. He was a knight from Herefordshire called Sir Peter de la Mare, a brave and outspoken man, who is generally considered to have been the first Speaker of the Commons.[15] After several days of discussion, the commons left the chapter house and went to meet the lords. It was now that Peter de la Mare presented their grievances. According to an eye-witness, this is what he said:

> My lords, we have come here before you, on your command, to show you what is grieving our hearts: and we say that we have declared to you, and to all the council of parliament, numerous crimes and extortions committed by various people; and we have had no redress. Nor are there any persons about the king who will tell the truth, or give him loyal and profitable counsel, but they mock, and they scoff, and they work always for their own profit. We declare to you, therefore, that we will do nothing further until those who are about the king, who are traitors and evil councillors, are dismissed from their offices: and until our lord king appoints as new members of his council men who will not shirk from telling the truth, and who will carry out reforms.[16]

That speech must have come as a bombshell to many of the lords. Nevertheless, the commons got almost everything they were asking for, at least for the time being. A dozen or so royal ministers and courtiers were impeached. (This was the first time that the procedure had been used in parliament. Essentially, it consisted of a prosecution by the commons, leading to judgement by the lords.) A new council was set up to advise the king and, even more significantly, no tax was granted. And that was the crucial point. Fifty years earlier, a speech like that from a member of the commons would have been unthinkable. And the reason why members of the commons had

4.10. Parliament of Henry VIII, showing the Speaker of the Commons

acquired the power to make this sort of demand was because of their control over taxation. They had gained a bargaining-counter. Potentially, at least, that was a powerful lever.

For the commons were summoned to parliament to do two things: first, to grant taxation, and secondly, to present petitions for reform.

Their petitions – their grievances, in effect – covered a whole range of matters: trade restrictions, manipulation of the coinage, law and order, the corruption of royal ministers, and so forth. Often, like Peter de la Mare, they were highly critical of the government. What is more they expected the king to listen to their complaints, and to offer some remedy: if he failed to do so, he might not be granted his taxes. 'Redress of grievances before grant of supply.' The rallying-cry of the seventeenth century parliamentarians could already be heard, even if only dimly, in the parliaments of the fourteenth century.

But we must be careful not to over-emphasise what might be called the confrontational aspect of medieval parliaments. There was certainly plenty of hard bargaining going on, but the general impression is of a high degree of co-operation between the king and his parliaments. The idea of 'party politics', with parliament as a sort of forum for institutionalised opposition to the government, really has no relevance to the middle ages. And it is important to recognise the limits even to the *potential* power of the commons. Parliaments only met on average for a few weeks each year, so for much of the rest of the time, the commons could safely be ignored. In the real decision-making processes, they played very little part. Kingship in late medieval England remained as personal as it had ever been; ideas of limited monarchy, or 'constitutional monarchy', were hardly born.[17]

Even so, the growth of parliament was an event of tremendous importance. It was in parliament that legislation was made, state trials were held, taxation was granted, and great matters were debated (though not often decided). And the development of the power of the commons was especially significant, because in the long-term it was the most important political legacy of late medieval England. It was important partly because it gave the knights and burgesses a secure and lasting role in national politics, and thus served to broaden the English political nation. But it was also important because the powers which the commons had won in the fourteenth and fifteenth centuries – powers won initially under the pressure of foreign war, and the king's ever-growing need for money to finance that war – were, in the course of time, to be developed and expanded, until the commons found themselves in a position to challenge even the king for political supremacy in England. It was not until the seventeenth century that a king of England attempted to undermine the role of the commons. And in the civil war that followed, it was the king who emerged as the loser.

Further Reading

R.G. Davies and J.H. Denton (eds), *The English Parliament in the Middle Ages* (Manchester, 1981); K. Fowler, *The Age of Plantagenet and Valois* (London, 1967); G.L. Harriss, *King, Parliament and Public Finance in England to 1369* (Oxford, 1975); M.H. Keen, *The Laws of War in the Late Middle Ages* (London, 1965); K.B. McFarlane, *The Nobility of Later Medieval England* (Oxford, 1973); M.C. Prestwich, *The Three Edwards: War and State in England 1272–1377* (London, 1980).

CHAPTER FIVE

The Triumph of Scotland

Alexander Grant

'Is there anything to which you would wish to draw my attention?'
'To the curious incident of the dog in the night-time.'
'The dog did nothing in the night-time!'
'That was the curious incident', remarked Sherlock Holmes.

(A. Conan Doyle, 'Silver Blaze' in his
Memoirs of Sherlock Holmes)

The dog that did not bark in the night gives a perfect text for discussing medieval Scotland's political history. In a British context, the main point is the importance of what did *not* happen. Medieval Scotland was not conquered, neither by the Normans, nor by Edward I and his successors; and it did not suffer the continuous conflicts found in England throughout the middle ages. This chapter examines why this was so, and seeks to demonstrate how – as with the dog in the night – Scotland's history yields valuable clues about the nature of medieval political society. It shows, for instance, how a country could evolve peacefully out of the 'Dark Ages' into the mainstream of west European life. It illustrates the consequences, such as the growth of strong national kingship and government, and the emergence of widespread national consciousness. And, perhaps most importantly, it demonstrates that successful medieval government did not depend so much upon centralised institutions and bureaucracies as, in the last resort, upon good relations between the crown and its prominent subjects, the 'political community'.

To begin with, why was there no Norman Conquest of Scotland – neither a sudden conquest, as in England, nor a piecemeal one, as in Wales and much of Ireland? One answer must be that the Norman kings of England did not see the need to conquer it. Scotland, being

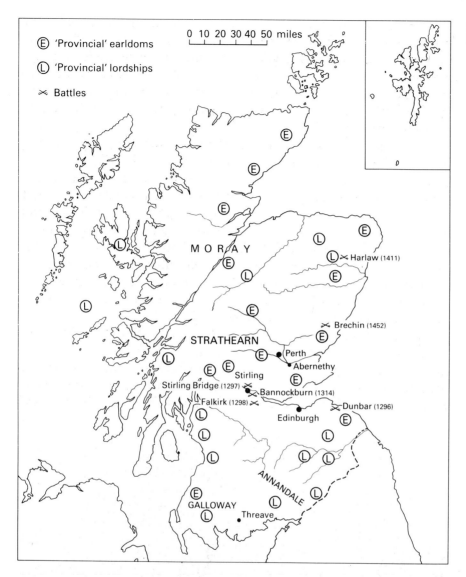

5.1. The Kingdom of Scotland

much poorer than England, was a far less attractive prize, not worth the effort of full-scale conquest. But Scottish raids on England did provoke William the Conqueror into invading Scotland in 1072, when the Scots king Malcolm III 'came and made peace with the king William, and gave hostages and became his man'.[1] After Malcolm's death in 1093, one of his sons, Edgar, gained the Scottish throne in 1097 with help from William Rufus, who treated Edgar as a client king. Clientage, not conquest, was what the two Williams wanted from Scotland. It gave them a reasonably secure northern border, and allowed them to concentrate on their chief priority, their lands in northern France. Then, after Henry I married a sister of Edgar in

1100, the Anglo-Scottish relationship became more equal. The marriage occurred because Henry wanted a link with the old Saxon royal house, from which Edgar and his sister were descended through their mother. It helped, however, to establish good relations between the English and Scottish crowns – good relations that lasted fairly well, despite occasional outbreaks of tension, for most of the twelfth and thirteenth centuries.

If the English kings did not want to conquer Scotland, what of their barons? The conquests in Wales and Ireland were largely the work of individual Norman barons, acting in their own private interests; they were successful because Wales and Ireland were highly fragmented, ruled by rival warring princes and kings, who could produce only limited resistance.[2] But Scotland had already developed into a relatively unified, powerful kingdom before any Normans appeared in the British Isles.[3] Although Malcolm III submitted temporarily to William the Conqueror, he would have had little difficulty in repelling attacks by individual Norman barons. Scotland was far less vulnerable to Norman adventurism than Wales or Ireland.

Yet while Scotland was not conquered, many Normans did in fact settle there. The influx started when Edgar's youngest brother, David, succeeded to the throne in 1124. Before becoming king, David had been prominent at the court of his brother-in-law, Henry I of England. There he had built up a sizeable following of Normans, Bretons and

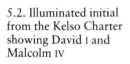

5.2. Illuminated initial from the Kelso Charter showing David I and Malcolm IV

Flemings, and many of these accompanied him to Scotland.

David I (1124–53) was one of Scotland's greatest kings. He brought Scotland up-to-date in twelfth century terms by, for instance, introducing the new reformed religious orders on a large scale, by creating new burghs and by issuing the first Scottish coinage. He greatly developed Scotland's government, along the lines of what he had experienced in England. And he established many of his followers permanently in Scotland. His grandsons Malcolm IV (1153–65) and William I (1165–1214) continued his policies. By the late twelfth century, Scotland had become a fairly typical west European kingdom; its government was similar to England's, if simpler, and its landowning aristocracy was extensively Normanised.[4]

It might therefore be argued that it does not matter that Scotland was not actually conquered by the Normans. But had that happened, British history would have been very different, for the kingdom of Scotland would have been dismantled, and the country would have come under English rule. Also, the Normanisation of Scotland did not involve any wholesale displacement of the native landowners. The incoming Normans were mostly endowed from crown lands, and simply fitted into the top level of Scottish society. By the 1180s a hybrid but homogeneous landowning society had evolved in Scotland: partly through intermarriage; partly because the native landowners adopted the feudal principles of land tenure introduced by David I and his Norman followers; and partly because all Scottish landowners, whatever their origins, owed allegiance to the king of Scots.[5] Scotland thus did not suffer from the racial divisions that characterise Welsh and Irish history.

Furthermore, because the Normans came into Scotland as followers of the Scottish kings, their well-nigh invincible military machinery, based on knights and castles, was used to support the Scottish crown, not destroy it. With it behind them, the twelfth and thirteenth century Scottish kings could always subdue or crush opposition. Previously, kings had frequently been overthrown and killed by rivals – in that respect, Shakespeare's *Macbeth* tells the truth. But Edgar, in 1097, was the last one to gain the Scottish throne by armed force. Thereafter, whenever kings faced rebellions or challenges (chiefly from the great northern province of Moray) they dealt with them easily. And military power at the crown's disposal enabled royal authority to be extended into the country's periphery. In the south-west Galloway was brought under control; in the north, Moray was subdued and shared among crown supporters; and, by the mid-thirteenth century, even the lords of the north-western seaboard were acknowledging the king's authority. The process culminated in 1266, when the king of Norway ceded the Western Isles to Alexander III, following the defeat of a Norwegian force three years earlier at Largs. This success illustrates the steady strengthening of Scottish kingship during the twelfth and thirteenth centuries – a strengthening based on the co-operation of crown and Normanised aristocracy. It is probably the most important legacy of David I's peaceful introduction of the Normans into Scotland.

The annexation of the Western Isles, however, was a high point for Scotland. Within thirty years disaster had struck, in the person of Edward I of England. By the late thirteenth century, the English crown was no longer involved in France, while Scotland (because of the wealth brought by wool exports)[6] had become a more attractive prize. Moreover, in the 1280s, Edward I had conquered the last independent part of Wales, and it was natural for him to maintain the momentum of conquest – especially when the tragic death of Alexander III (1249–86) brought the direct line of Scottish kings to a sudden end. Edward was asked to adjudicate in the succession crisis that eventually followed Alexander's death. He did so in the 'Great Cause' of 1291–2 which found, correctly, in favour of John Balliol of Galloway, who duly became king in 1292.[7] Before adjudicating, however, Edward had insisted on being recognised as overlord of Scotland. The Scots reluctantly agreed, seeing that as a lesser evil than civil war. But after 1292 Edward set about trying to exercise full sovereignty over Scotland by, for instance, hearing Scottish litigation at Westminster, and demanding military service from Scottish nobles. This provoked general Scottish opposition, and war broke out – perhaps as Edward had anticipated. In 1296, he invaded Scotland, routed the Scottish host at Dunbar, made King John Balliol abdicate, and received submissions from some 2,000 Scottish landowners. As a clerk in his entourage put it, Edward 'conquered the kingdom of Scotland and searched it through . . . in twenty-one weeks and no more'.[8]

But while Edward I's conquest of Wales proved permanent, his conquest of Scotland did not. Scottish resistance, initially led by Andrew Murray and William Wallace, flared up in 1297 and from then on, despite campaigns in 1298, 1300, 1301 and 1303–4, Edward never managed to force total, lasting Scottish submission. After his death in 1307, the Scots, now with the great Robert Bruce (1306–29) as their king,[9] removed the English hold on Scotland altogether. Robert defeated an English army in pitched battle at Bannockburn in 1314, and forced English recognition of Scottish independence by the treaty of Edinburgh of 1328.[10] And although, following Robert's death, Edward III of England broke the treaty in the 1330s, his efforts also eventually came to nothing. The English kings never renounced their claims on Scotland, and sporadic Anglo-Scottish warfare continued, but by the later fourteenth century Scottish independence was safe.

Why did the Scots manage to maintain their independence when the Welsh failed? There are many reasons, including Scotland's size and geography, Robert I's military genius, French diplomatic support and the renewed English warfare in France after 1337. The main point, however, is that Wales and Scotland are not really comparable. Edward I did not conquer the whole of Wales, but simply the north-west; the rest had already been conquered by Anglo-Norman magnates.[11] All Edward I did was complete the final stage of the Norman conquest of Wales. The Scottish parallel is the final stage of the Normanisation of Scotland: Alexander III's extension of his authority into the north-west during the 1260s and 1270s. In a British context, Edward I's attack on Scotland was something quite new. He was attempting to conquer another Normanised kingdom in which the Normanised ruling class did not support the English crown, as the Anglo-Norman landowners in Wales did, but provided the backbone of the Scottish resistance.

This is crucial, because conquest is not simply about winning battles; victories must be consolidated. Edward I's conquest of north-west Wales was consolidated by the Anglo-Norman landowners, who already controlled most of Wales, and were entrusted with much of the newly-conquered territory.[12] But how could Edward I consolidate his apparent conquest of Scotland? He had two alternatives: to replace thousands of Scottish landowners with English ones, or to gain widespread Scottish collaboration. The former would have been an extremely difficult undertaking; the latter would have seemed much easier, especially when so many Scots submitted in 1296. As Edward found out, however, the Scots could neither be trusted nor forced to collaborate permanently. No simple explanation exists for this; individual Scots had individual motives for opposing English rule, and few showed absolute consistency. Nevertheless, there were two decisive factors which encouraged enough Scots to fight for enough of the time to ensure ultimate Scottish victory in the long struggle with England.

First there is the ideology of Scottish independence. Over the twelfth and thirteenth centuries, a distinct sense of Scottishness developed within the political community – the hybrid but Normanised land-owning class. It focused chiefly on the king, but also engendered a distinct concept of the kingdom. This is evident from the great seal cut for the 'guardians' who governed Scotland after Alexander III's death. Instead of the usual portrayals of the king, it showed the lion rampant (Scotland's heraldic device) and St Andrew, with the legends, 'The Seal of Scotland appointed for the government of the kingdom' and

5.3. The seal of the
Guardians of Scotland
showing St Andrew

'Andrew be leader of the compatriot Scots'.[13] In 1304, the defenders
of Stirling Castle said they held it 'of the Lion'. This abstract concept
of Scotland and Scotland's interests lay behind the original revolt
against Edward I in 1296; it provided an essential stimulus and
rallying-point for those brave or recalcitrant enough to fight against
the might of England in the following decades; and in 1320, it reached
its full development in that dramatic articulation of Scottish
independence, the Declaration of Arbroath. The Declaration stated,

> Yet if he [Robert I] should give up what he has begun, seeking to
> make us or our kingdom subject to the king of England or to the
> English, we would strive at once to drive him out as our enemy and
> a subverter of his own right and ours, and we would make some
> other man who was able to defend us our king; for as long as a
> hundred of us remain alive, we will never on any condition be
> subjected to the lordship of the English.[14]

Secondly, there is the military factor. After Edward I had crushed
the Normanised Scottish host at Dunbar, the leaders of the fresh
Scottish resistance worked out new methods of waging war, using foot

5.4. The Declaration of Arbroath

5.5. The seal of King Robert I

soldiers armed with long pikes. In 1297, Andrew Murray and William Wallace successfully ambushed an English army at Stirling Bridge (where Murray was mortally wounded); and in 1298, although Edward heavily defeated Wallace's force at Falkirk, Wallace's pikemen did withstand repeated cavalry charges. Medieval infantry usually fled when charged by armoured knights; Wallace was among the first commanders to solve the problem. He arranged his men in 'schiltroms', or massed circles, wooden stakes hammered into the ground in front of them, and the stakes tied together – in other words, he roped them in![15] That, unfortunately, left his schiltroms vulnerable to archers. Nevertheless, it is clear that the Scots had developed an effective means of combating the cavalry might of England, which Robert I perfected. At Bannockburn, his pikemen, fighting in more fluid schiltroms on carefully chosen ground, dealt with the English cavalry host, while his light horsemen scattered the English archers. But even more typical is his brilliant guerilla strategy (later known as 'Good King Robert's testament'), in which the Scots did not confront English invasions head-on, but harried them, attacked their communications, and applied scorched-earth tactics, thus forcing their withdrawal – leaving the Scots free to pick off the various English-held strongholds.

The actual fighting was done by the ordinary people; the pikemen came mostly from the substantial peasantry. They fought without pay: the armies of the Wars of Independence were simply raised through the fundamental obligation of national defence (which spared the Scots the crippling expenses incurred by the English crown on army wages). Thus Scotland's military system can be described as 'popular'. But the organisation and leadership, without which armies are mere rabbles, came from the Normanised Scottish landowners. Wallace, though a minor country squire, belonged to that class, while Murray and Bruce were from the ranks of the magnates. This was no coincidence. Norman military success had been based on leadership and organisation as well as on armoured cavalry; now, in Scotland, these vital qualities were used to counter the hitherto invincible (in Britain at least) armies of English knights. This is a crucial difference with Wales and Ireland, where the way to wage war successfully against the English was never found. It was the Normanised Scottish landowners in whom the Scottish military effort found its all-important leaders (nowadays the 'officer corps') who achieved that vital breakthrough.

After the triumphs of the independence struggle, Scottish history in the rest of the middle ages was traditionally regarded as an anti-climax, characterised by the 'melancholy repetition'[16] of violent conflicts

5.6. A fifteenth century
impression of the battle
of Bannockburn

5.7. James II, King of Scots

between under-mighty kings and over-mighty magnates. This view is remarkably tenacious, but recent work proves it to be completely mistaken,[17] and it should be expunged from the Scottish historical consciousness.

When fourteenth and fifteenth century Scotland is put into a British context, political violence turns out to have been relatively infrequent.[18] Although James I (1406–37) was assassinated and James III (1460–88) was killed in battle against rebels, in England five kings were killed during the two centuries, and the crown changed hands violently seven times. In Scotland there were fifteen revolts and conspiracies, in England there were thirty-two. In Scotland (outside the Wars of Independence) there were ten pitched battles and skirmishes, in England at least twenty-three. And among the Scottish magnate class (which was similar in size to the English), twenty-two individuals met politically related deaths in battle, in custody or on the scaffold, whereas in England the total was no fewer than eighty! The contrast is not only with England; comparisons with France, Spain and Italy would give similar results.

Furthermore, in Scotland acts of political violence were generally followed by reconciliation, not by revenge and fresh violence. When the 1363 rebellion against David II (1329–71) by three great earls collapsed due to lack of support and decisive royal action, David merely demanded the rebels' submissions and promises of future loyalty. After the revolt of the Lord of the Isles in 1411 had been checked at the bloody battle of Harlaw (Aberdeenshire), the government expedition of the following year simply enforced his submission. And when in 1451, James II (1437–60) came into conflict with his greatest magnate, William, eighth earl of Douglas, parliament persuaded James to back down, 'And all gud scottismen war rycht blyth [happy] of that accordance'.[19] Exceptionally, however, that settlement did not last. In 1452 a fresh quarrel flared up, and during a private meeting in Stirling Castle, King James killed Earl William in a fit of temper. Three years later, he attacked the dead earl's brothers, bombarded the great Douglas castle of Threave, in Galloway, into submission, and finally crushed the house of Douglas. Yet even here the basic pattern applies. When his brothers tried to retaliate after Earl William's death, they could only raise six hundred followers. And although one of Earl William's confederates, the earl of Crawford, revolted in the north-east, he was defeated at Brechin by the earl of Huntly:

> And thair was with the erll of huntlie fer ma [more] than was with the erll of craufurd becauss he displayit the kingis banere And said it was the kingis actioun And he was his luftennend.[20]

Apart from Crawford, the only Scottish magnate to side with the Douglases was Lord Hamilton; he was reconciled with James in 1455 and finished up high in royal favour. Thus the James II–Douglas conflict – the nearest Scottish equivalent to England's Wars of the Roses – did not affect the whole political community and caused no more than a few months' disturbance. Despite its dramas, it helps to demonstrate the essentially low-key nature of late medieval Scottish politics.

Why did late medieval Scotland's political society have these characteristics? The main answers probably lie in the areas of central government and local power.[21] First, although Scotland's system of government had been largely copied from England by David I and his successors, the institutions were never so highly developed and centralised. They did not need to be: England's centralisation was mostly caused by the pressure of continual foreign wars. In Scotland, the chancery, the exchequer and the king's private staff were relatively small; the only central courts, apart from parliament and the royal council, were those held by two justiciars (chief justices); the armies were raised through a simple *levée en masse*; and (largely because military costs were so low) the crown managed on a yearly revenue of between about £5,000 and £10,000 sterling, roughly a tenth of that of the English crown. That does not mean that Scotland was necessarily badly governed. The two main tasks of government, national defence and internal order, were achieved at least as well as anywhere else. But in Scotland, the responsibility for these tasks lay chiefly in the localities, with the major landowners. They acted as sheriffs (the crown's main local agents); they raised and led armies; and they administered most of the country's justice in the sheriff courts and, within their own estates, in their barony and regality courts.

Secondly, in the localities, the great magnates mostly controlled large, coherent territorial units. Their main estates and followings tended to be concentrated in specific areas, not scattered across the country, as in England. From before the arrival of the Normans until the early fifteenth century, much of Scotland was covered by a network of earldoms and great lordships, each stretching over hundreds of square miles and roughly corresponding to provinces of the country. Good examples include the earldom of Strathearn, containing the broad valley of the river Earn south-west of Perth and extending westwards beyond Loch Earn, and the lordship of Annandale (given by David I to the Bruces) running north-west from the Border near Carlisle to the watershed with Clydesdale. Within them, the earls and lords wielded extensive authority, and this imposed a highly regionalised pattern on the country's landowning structure. And although, for various reasons, the network of earldoms and lordships disintegrated in the fifteenth century, the regionalised pattern of local power continued to exist. Many fifteenth century magnates developed clear-cut, effective spheres of influence, based on their relationship with the local lairds, or gentry. Leading magnates usually had close, exclusive relationships with neighbouring lairds; the latter either were cadets of the magnates' families, and so were bound by the obligations of kinship, or had established similar obligations by giving written promises of loyal, exclusive service, known as 'bonds of manrent'. In the north-east, the power built up by the Gordon earls of Huntly brought them the nickname 'Cock o' the North'; in the south-west, in Ayrshire and Galloway,

> 'Twixt Wigton and the town of Ayr,
> Port Patrick and the Cruives of Cree,
> No man needs think for to bide there
> Unless he court with Kennedie.[22]

According to the traditional, gloomy view of medieval Scotland, underdeveloped central institutions and strong local magnate power caused great problems. But the lesson of modern work is the opposite:

these factors were major reasons for Scotland's political stability.[23] For example, since the Scots crown did not challenge the magnates' local power, but accepted it as an integral part of the country's system of government, Scotland was spared an important source of crown–noble tension. Also, the lack of strong centralised institutions made it virtually impossible for the kings or their courtiers to manipulate the machinery of government for partisan ends. And because the crown did not have much money, there was little competition among magnates to gain financial patronage and divert crown revenue into their own coffers. In the localities, where individual magnates had these clear-cut spheres of influence, violent disputes between magnates for the control of particular areas were not very common, and it was difficult for feuding lairds to play one magnate off against another. Magnate power was normally used to settle feuding, and so maintain the peace. Moreover, what feuding there was generally did not escalate beyond limited areas. Similarly, because the institutional links between the centre and localities were not very strong, political disputes at the centre tended not to radiate outwards.

The result was that the political community as a whole was insulated from the effects of power struggles, either at the centre or in the localities – and that, therefore, if full-scale conflict did break out between the king and a magnate, most members of the political community would have had no reason to oppose the crown.[24] That was the case even in the deadly conflict between James II and the Douglases. In the much more centralised England, in contrast, both central and local conflicts tended to embroil large sections of the political community – often with disastrous results.[25]

These generally good relations between the crown and political community had their formal expression in the Scottish parliament. The great central institution of parliament stops Scotland from being regarded as a decentralised kingdom. Parliament was the supreme legislative, judicial, fiscal and administrative body – the forum where king and political community met together to discuss and determine whatever the kingdom's interests required. In fact, parliament had exactly the same constitutional position in Scotland as in England. Yet the history of the Scottish parliament is very different. The general conclusions about Scotland's stability apply strongly here. The constitutional crises which punctuate English parliamentary history are conspicuous by their absence. That was not because the Scots parliament was powerless. It was perfectly prepared to stand up to the king when necessary. In 1368 it stated that 'it was not expedient to the community' to impose any direct taxation the following year, and in the 1420s and 1430s it resisted several taxation demands. In 1370 it enacted that royal instructions to officials which broke the law were to be null and void, and in 1388 it had one of the king's sons dismissed as justiciar because he was 'useless to the community'.[26] These examples echo the issues that were so common in England, but very faintly. Co-operation, not confrontation, was the norm in the Scottish parliament.

This brings the basic nature of Scottish kingship back into view. In general, kings did not make great demands of their people, and did not antagonise their political communities. In particular, because they never had to pay their armies and did not fight wars abroad, they had far less need than the English crown to demand taxation. Earlier historians have often lamented the absence of regular, direct taxation in Scotland; medieval Scots would hardly have agreed. The fundamental point is that the Scottish crown was never oppressive or predatory. This applies throughout the middle ages: from the reign of David I and the Normanisation of Scotland, past the reign of Robert I and the time of the Wars of Independence, and on to the reign of

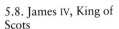

5.8. James IV, King of Scots

James IV in the early Renaissance. For most of this period, Scotland enjoyed what was by contemporary standards good and effective government, based not so much on institutional centralisation as on the close co-operation of the kings and the political community. During the middle ages, indeed, Scotland's kingship and political life should be regarded as one of the great success stories of European history.

Further Reading

G.W.S. Barrow, *Robert Bruce and the Community of the Realm of Scotland* (Edinburgh, 1976); G.W.S. Barrow, *Kingship and Unity: Scotland 1000–1306* (London, 1981); J.M. Brown, *Scottish Society in the Fifteenth Century* (London, 1977); W.C. Dickinson, *Scotland from Earliest Times to 1603*, revised by A.A.M. Duncan (Oxford, 1977); A.A.M. Duncan, *Scotland: The Making of the Kingdom* (Edinburgh, 1975); A. Grant, *Independence and Nationhood: Scotland 1306–1469* (London, 1984); R. Nicholson, *Scotland: The Later Middle Ages* (Edinburgh, 1974); J. Wormald, *Court, Kirk and Community: Scotland 1470–1625* (London, 1981).

CHAPTER
SIX

Working the Land

David Carpenter

The map of rural England today is studded with villages, many only two or three miles apart, and the great majority of these villages have existed since Domesday Book was compiled in 1086. Within them, in the middle ages, lived over ninety per cent of the population. Even in the 1980s English villages have much to remind us of their medieval origins – the church most frequently and often parts of a manor house or castle, the lay-out of the streets and cottages, and features in the fields. The English village landscape of today was made in the middle ages.

One interesting example is the village of Willingham, some seven miles north of Cambridge.[1] Here the church was built between the thirteenth and fifteenth centuries: inside, the pulpit, rood screen, chancel stalls and wall paintings – the best preserved is of St Christopher – all belong to the same period. The manor house was next to the church, and its foundations are sometimes revealed when graves are dug in the churchyard.

None of the cottages of Willingham is earlier than 1600, but the basic form of the village is very much a product of the medieval period. The village was probably laid out by its medieval lord, the bishop of Ely. Its three streets and the plots of land in which the cottages stand are all found on a map of 1575, which also shows that in the middle ages the arable land of the village was grouped to the east in three large open fields. Although these were divided into smaller fields and orchards in the nineteenth century, tracks and footpaths still indicate their old boundaries.

Many other villages, more fortunate than Willingham, have preserved part or all of the medieval manor house. At Broughton in Oxfordshire, for example, the fortified house, with its superb vaulted passage ways and private chapel, is still inhabited, while the church

6.1. Interior of
Willingham Church

6.2. Sixteenth century
plan of Willingham

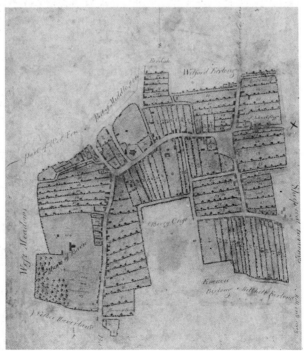

6.3. Broughton Castle

6.4. The founders of
Broughton Castle

contains the effigies of its builders, the knights who were lords of the manor.[2] There are other striking manor houses at Layer Marney (Essex), Ockwells (Berkshire), and South Wraxhall (Wiltshire).[3] It is much more difficult to discover the remains of the cottages of the medieval peasants. This is because they were made of wood, and were reconstructed from one generation to the next. One house at Wharram Percy in Yorkshire was rebuilt nine times between the 1190s and the 1500s. Excavations on the sites of deserted villages show that such cottages usually consisted of a single long room, with the long side facing onto the village street. The room was divided into two portions, one for the stable, the other, with a hearth in the centre, as living quarters.[4]

There are many villages, like Willingham, or Cuxham (Oxfordshire), East Witton (Yorkshire), and Laxton (Nottinghamshire), where the basic lay-out is demonstrably of medieval origin. At Laxton, the great open fields characteristic of medieval farming have escaped the process of enclosure into smaller fields, which was general in England between the fifteenth and nineteenth centuries.[5] Elsewhere, although the land has been enclosed, one can often see, bisected by the later hedges, the shape of the open fields and the ridges and furrows created by centuries of medieval ploughing. In its destruction of the hedgerows modern farming practice has done something to restore the landscape to its medieval appearance.

Although many villages look much the same today as they did in the middle ages, the pattern of rural life then was very different. At the heart of that life was the land itself, which produced the corn essential for everyone's existence. The inequitable distribution of the land beween lords and peasants, together with the system by which the land was cultivated, created the class structure of medieval England, and determined that lords lived in grand manor houses which sometimes still survive, and peasants in tiny wooden cottages which have vanished. The institution which governed the distribution and cultivation of the land had developed before 1066. It was called the manor.

In a village organised as a manor all the land in the fields was the lord's; a large part he kept in his own hands – his demesne: the rest was held from him by peasants in return for working on the demesne, and giving him rents in money and in kind. At Cuxham in Oxfordshire in 1086, for example, the lord retained around 200 acres of land as demesne. The seven most prosperous peasants had individual holdings of about twelve acres. In return for them, they owed services: providing a man to work on the lord's demesne on alternate days throughout the year, with two extra men at time of harvest; ploughing and harrowing a quarter of an acre of demesne; and at Christmas, giving the lord 6d or a cock, two hens and two loaves of bread.[6]

Although land remained the basis of life throughout the middle ages, there was nothing static about the social system which we have just described. On the contrary, in the period between the Norman Conquest and the sixteenth century, it changed dramatically. That period is sharply divided by the Black Death of 1348–9. In the years between 1066 and 1349 the economic and social position of the peasantry gravely deteriorated. Increasing numbers of villagers found themselves living on the verge of subsistence, and literally starving to death in years of bad harvest. At the same time, those peasants who owed labour services became villeins, that is unfree men, tied to their manors, deprived of access to the king's courts, and subject in nearly all respects to the will of their lords. After 1349 all this changed. The economic and social position of the peasantry improved vastly as the spectre of starvation was banished; peasants ceased to perform labour services and instead held their land in return for moderate money rents. The old restrictions of villeinage fell away. Peasants in practice became free men. Essentially, these changes were determined by three interrelated factors. The period between 1066 and 1349 was characterised by first, a sharply rising population; secondly, a close involvement of lords in the running of their manors; and thirdly, a muted level of peasant protest. In the period after 1349 all three trends went into sharp reverse. The population fell drastically; lords ceased to be involved in manorial administration; peasant protest was widespread.

I now propose to consider in more detail how these factors caused the changes I have mentioned, and to begin first with the period between 1066 and 1349. Here it was the first factor, the great rise in the population, which was responsible for bringing the threat of famine to many peasant homes.

England's population probably multiplied nearly fourfold between 1086 and 1349, from 1.6 million to around six million. At Taunton,

6.5. Breaking the land

6.6. Ploughing the land

6.7. Clearing the forest

for example, the number of adult males doubled in the thirteenth century in three generations alone. At Spalding (Lincolnshire) there were ninety-one households in 1081 and 587 in 1287.[7] Wasteland was cleared, and marshes drained to provide more land for the new population. The Lincolnshire fens for example, were brought into cultivation. But there was a limit to which this could be done. A large section of the new population was composed of smallholders, people who possessed under (usually well under) ten acres of land. Thus at Cuxham the increase was greatest amongst peasants with at most one and a half acres of land – there were four in 1086, thirteen in 1279.[8] By contrast, in the same period, the number of more prosperous peasants, those with twelve acres of land, rose by only one. By 1279 some forty per cent of England's peasant population were smallholders.

The central fact to appreciate is that men could not support their families entirely from their land. Given the inefficiency of medieval agriculture, at least ten acres was necessary in the thirteenth century to ensure a family bare subsistence. In order to live, therefore, small holders had to buy corn on the market. They obtained the money to do so by working as wage labourers for lords and wealthier peasants. The state of the harvest each year determined the price of corn and for those at the lower end of the scale, the cost of corn was absolutely crucial. If the harvest was bad, and scarcity sent prices soaring up, the smallholder might be unable to buy enough to live. In years of bad harvest like 1258 so many villagers died of starvation that their bodies lay unburied around the streets. England resembled a third-world country of today. Hunger was ever present, and many, with emaciated bodies, hollow cheeks and staring eyes, eked out an anxious existence from one harvest to the next.[9]

The second determining factor between 1066 and 1349 was the

6.8. Gathering the harvest

growing interest of the lords in the running of their manors. This change in attitude deprived the peasants of their legal freedom and turned them into villeins. Lords began to give their attention to manorial administration around 1150. At that time, the price of corn, fuelled by the demand of the rising population, began an inflationary spiral which continued into the fourteenth century. To take advantage of this bouyant market, lords attempted to increase their profits by producing more corn for sale. They expanded the area of their demesnes and exploited them more intensely. To do this effectively they needed all the labour they could get and it became vital to establish control and discipline over their peasant workforce. Thus, in the years after 1150, lords, working hand in hand with the compliant lawyers of the king, began to impose the components of unfreedom. Whether or not a peasant carried out labour services for the lord became the touchstone. It was laid down that anyone who performed services could not leave the manor or buy or sell land without his lord's permission. In addition, he could bring no legal actions in the king's courts to defend himself against his lord's demands and depredations. Thus the villein, for this was the name given to the unfree, lived at the mercy of his lord. Between England's free and unfree population there was a rigid dividing line.[10]

The third determining factor before 1349 was the absence of any serious movements of peasant protest. This made it possible for the lord to impose and maintain the restrictions of villeinage which we have described. People certainly refused to perform labour services, and sometimes peasants attempted to prove at law that they were not villeins. But these were isolated incidents, easily resisted. Above all, peasants were quite unable to take what, in any period, was the most effective of all routes of protest – that of leaving the manor if they did not like their lord's terms. The rising population and the dearth of land simply meant that there was no possibility of finding land and livelihood elsewhere. Thus, increasingly, economic trends fortified legal restrictions in making peasants captives of their lords. The latter were able to impose their own conditions with confidence. In the thirteenth century one peasant, rather than accept land on terms of villeinage, declared that he would commit suicide, and he did so, drowning himself in the River Severn.[11] From the manor there was no other form of escape.

Let us now turn to the momentous improvements in the conditions of the peasantry in the period after the Black Death. These were caused by a transformation of the three determining factors operating before 1349. The population now fell dramatically; lords ceased to be concerned with the running of their manors; and peasant protest became extensive. As a result, the threat of famine evaporated; labour services were replaced by rents; and the restrictions of villeinage disappeared.

The dramatic fall in the population was brought about by the Black Death, a devastating combination of bubonic and pneumonic plague. Bubonic plague begins when the bacterium *pasteurella pestis* invades rats and causes plague amongst the rat population. The disease is then transferred from rats to humans by the rat flea. In man its termination

6.9. Victims of the Black Death

6.10. Sowing seed

is fatal in ninety per cent of cases in the initial weeks of an epidemic.
Plague rats reached England in June 1348. Fleas travelled easily about
the human person; rats were transported in corn coming and going
from markets. Since most villages were only a few miles apart, the
disease spread quickly. Bubonic plague, moreover, was soon accompanied by the more deadly pneumonic variety. Unlike bubonic plague,
this can last throughout the winter; it has a consistent death rate of
one hundred per cent, and is communicated from person to person in
the breath – hence the nursery rhyme, 'attishoo, attishoo, all fall
down'. Studies of individual villages reveal the horrific nature of the
attack of 1348, which the pneumonic variant continued throughout
the winter into 1349. At Cuxham it killed two-thirds of the

population. At Bishops Waltham in Hampshire, seven people died in 1346 and fourteen in 1347, the two years immediately preceding the plague. In the year 1348–9, 264 people died.[12] After 1349 rats in England were never wholly free of the bubonic bacterium, and between 1361 and 1485 there were twelve more national outbreaks of plague (the last great outbreak in London was as late as 1665–6). The Black Death of 1348–9 probably reduced the population by almost half, certainly by one third. The subsequent plagues were less severe, but they effectively prevented any recovery in numbers.[13]

The chief consequence of such a drastic reduction in population was to lift the threat of starvation from the peasantry. This threat had pressed most heavily on the peasant smallholders, the men who lacked the land to support their families, and worked as wage labourers. Their situation now altered out of all recognition. The fall in population meant that instead of land being scarce it was now available in abundance. Numerous smallholders were able to step into vacated peasant holdings of between ten and thirty acres. Thus for the first time they acquired land extensive enough to support their families. We can see this taking place at Cuxham. The Black Death had killed all the peasants with twelve-acre holdings. Three small-holders, with only one and a half acres, had survived and, by 1352, each of these had acquired one of the twelve-acre tenements.[14] Even for those peasants who did not acquire land sufficient for subsistence, and remained instead as wage labourers, life took on a rosier hue. Since the upward movement of smallholders had created a great dearth of labour, they were able to obtain much higher wages. A study of wage levels on the manors of the bishopric of Winchester and the abbey of Westminster shows that between 1311 and 1350 wages had held steady at well under 2d per day for a labourer. In the decade after the Black Death they rose to 2·85d per day; by 1391–1400 they stood at 3·30d per day and by 1441–50 at nearly 5d.[15] Given declining prices, the value of wages in real terms probably doubled by the 1390s and tripled by the 1440s.

The second determining factor after 1349 was the gradual withdrawal of lords from the running of their manors. This cleared the way for the replacement of labour services by rents, and the ending of the restrictions of villeinage. The economic background to the change was produced by the falling population which meant a lower demand for corn, and so the price fell from the high levels of the thirteenth century. Since there were no longer ever-increasing profits to be made by selling corn on the market, lords were no longer tied to demesne farming. They could consider leasing the demesne and living off the rents. If the latter were kept at a reasonable level and tenants could be attracted easily, the lord, on his part, had less need to maintain general control over his peasants. This in turn might weaken the restrictions of villeinage. Some lords reacted quickly to the new economic conditions. At Cuxham the demesne was leased as early as 1356, and the 12s 6d annual rents for the twelve-acre tenements were more than 8s lower than the value of the labour services which they replaced. Some other lords, however, were slow to recognise the logic of the economic situation. Their initial reaction after the Black Death was conservative and repressive. Some stuck to demesne farming and tried to enforce villeinage and labour services – the latter were exacted in full down to 1390 on the lands of Canterbury cathedral priory – others abandoned labour services and tried to force peasants to stay on their manors and pay heavy money rents. With these lords the third determining factor becomes important, for the strength of peasant protest after 1349 provided them with a powerful incentive to change their ways.

The most striking incident of peasant protest was the Great Revolt of 1381. With its central demands for the abolition of labour services and villeinage, and for rents of 4d an acre, it was provoked by precisely the conservative reaction of these landlords.[16] Less spectacular, but in the long run more effective, were the local struggles which

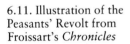

6.11. Illustration of the Peasants' Revolt from Froissart's *Chronicles*

peasants waged with their lords. In manor after manor they demanded and frequently secured better terms: moderate rents, for example, to replace labour services; the right to sell their land; and the protection against the arbitrary will of the lord afforded by holding that land under the terms of a fixed, written agreement. The great bargaining weapon for the peasant was the threat to leave the manor, in which case the lord would find himself with a deserted and worthless village. Before 1349, the threat to leave was vain because there was nowhere else for the peasant to go. After 1349, it was a powerful weapon.

The legal restrictions tying the peasants to the manor no longer corresponded with economic realities. There was plenty of land for them elsewhere. At Hatton in Warwickshire, the peasants, disliking the high rents which had replaced labour services and the continued restrictions of villeinage, voted steadily with their feet, so that between the 1370s and 1428 the village became totally depopulated. Probably many of them settled in the neighbouring village of Hampton Lucy where there was no villeinage, and rents were low.[17] In the same way the attractive rents at Cuxham drew peasants from outside the manor, and may have contributed to the depopulation of the neighbouring villages of Clare and Easington where labour services may have persisted. By the fifteenth century, therefore, the peasant's position had been transformed. Labour services had been replaced almost universally by rents, which were usually set at a moderate figure. Peasants were emerging from the confines of villeinage; it was no longer possible to bind them to the manor; in addition, they were beginning to hold their land under the terms of an agreement with their lords copied in the manor records; an agreement which fixed the rents and guaranteed the right to sell the land. By the 1450s the king's courts were starting to protect the security of this 'copyhold' tenure. No longer menaced by famine, provided they could escape the recurrent bouts of plague, the peasants were entering their golden age.

Something of the assertiveness and self-confidence of the peasants of this period can be seen in Wat Tyler of Maidstone, the leader of the rebels in 1381. Tyler was a quick-tempered, violent, vulgar man – 'the greatest thief and robber in all Kent' as one enemy called him. It is not surprising that there is no statue to him in Maidstone. Yet he had a wonderful arrogance, and a profound sense of the strength and importance of the movement which he led. When he met the young King Richard II at Smithfield, he dismounted from his horse, but did not doff his cap; he took the king by the arm, and shook it roughly in greeting; called him comrade, and refused with a great oath to dismiss his men, promising that in two weeks there would be forty thousand more of them. As he put his demands to Richard, he threw a dagger from hand to hand, and then rinsed out his mouth from a jug of water and took a swig from a flagon of ale. Here, indeed, was a peasant who could talk on equal terms with a king![18]

In his brief moment of glory, Wat Tyler comes alive for us as a person. Where, indeed, we can glean information about the private activities and personalities of medieval peasants, we are reminded that human beings are the same everywhere, whatever the differences of the social systems in which they live. And, just as there is physically much continuity between the medieval village and the village of today, so, in the lives of the medieval villagers there is much that is recognisable. Then, as now, life in the village could revolve around the church and the tavern. Sayings like 'He recovered from his illness and went as usual to the church and tavern' were common. The tavern or, as we might call it, the pub, was usually kept in a villager's house. After sports such as wrestling, archery, forms of football, rugger, and hockey, it was the custom to repair there for beer or ale. Too much alcohol was often consumed, and there were many drunken fights. In 1254, a pint pot full of beer brought down on an opponent's head proved a lethal weapon. Another fight in the same year began when a drunken carter ran down a group of men just out of the ale house, themselves drunk, singing in the road. Women also featured in pub life. At Acton Scott in Shropshire on Christmas Day 1284, the men went out of the tavern to sing to women standing opposite in the field. A few years before, a great brawl began when Thomas Kauke accused Margaret Totwell of frequenting the tavern with lecherous intent. Thomas's wife, Mabel, came to blows with Margaret, and was thrown out onto the street, only to return with her son to wreak havoc and vengeance.

But the medieval villagers could also show warm love and affection. When Henry of Bretteby killed his son out ploughing, the jury were sure it was an accident: 'they know for a truth that Henry would rather have killed himself than his only son.' When Ughtred Smith was struck on the head by an arrow he insisted on pulling it out before he went home 'so that my wife may not see it for she would perhaps be excessively alarmed'. Between friends in the village there could also be much humour. In 1267, William of Stansgate, carrying bow and arrows, met the widow Desiderata, a particular friend and his child's godmother, in the street. She asked him in jest if he was one of the men appointed by the king to keep the peace and, declaring she could overcome two or three like him, crooked her leg, grabbed him by the neck and threw him to the ground![19]

In the village today let us certainly explore the remains of the manor house, and in the church, inspect the effigies of the knights who lived there. But let us also look for the sites of the peasants' cottages, discover the remains of the open fields in which the peasants worked, and remember the vast number of villagers who lived hidden lives and now rest in unmarked graves.

Further Reading

H.S. Bennett, *Life on the English Manor* (Cambridge, 1938); J.L. Bolton, *The Medieval English Economy 1150–1500* (London, 1980); P.D.A. Harvey, *A Medieval Oxfordshire Village: Cuxham 1240–1400* (Oxford, 1965); R.H. Hilton, *A Medieval Society. The West Midlands at the End of the Thirteenth Century* (London, 1966); W.G. Hoskins, *The Making of the English Landscape*, 2nd edn (London, 1977); J.Z. Titow, *English Rural Society 1200–1350* (London, 1969).

CHAPTER SEVEN

The Lords of the Manor

Caroline Barron

John Paston, a country gentleman from Norfolk, died in 1466 while staying at an inn in London. This was not an event of great importance in a city where many people died every day, but in his home village of Paston on the windswept Norfolk coast, and among the prosperous manor houses of that fertile county, it was an event of great significance. The Pastons were wealthy (later it became a commonplace that you never saw a poor Paston), and, while normally tightfisted, on this occasion they saw fit to display their wealth. The corpse was carried home from London escorted by twelve poor men bearing torches. It rested at Norwich, and then moved on to the priory of Bromholm where John was buried in the place of honour next to Sir William Glanville who had founded the priory in 1113.[1] Now, three hundred years later, the Pastons were taking over Bromholm as its second founders. The Paston servants and the household of the prior of Bromholm had been working for days killing beasts, brewing beer and cooking geese and chickens in preparation for the funeral feast. The guests also consumed a thousand eggs, twenty gallons of milk, forty-one pigs and forty-nine calves. The smoke from the hundreds of candles, tapers and torches burning at the funeral dirge was so dense that a glazier had to be summoned to take out two of the windows of the priory church.[2] The coffin was covered with a rich cloth of gold although a stone tombchest was not erected over the grave for some years.[3] After Bromholm priory was dissolved in 1536, John Paston's tomb was transferred to the parish church, where it is now placed at the east end and serves as the altar.

There were many families like the Pastons in fifteenth century England; wealthy, tough and unscrupulous, of considerable influence in their localities and of growing importance in national politics. Some might become particularly rich and powerful, like the Woodvilles,

adiutor eorum + protector eorum est.
Domus aaron sperauit in domino:
adiutor eorum + protector eorum est.
Qui timent dominum sperauerunt

7.1a. Preparing food for the household

who supplied a queen of England in Elizabeth, the wife of Edward IV, and such men would serve as members of the king's council and be in frequent attendance at court. But scores of lesser gentlemen provided a

7.2. John Paston's tomb, now used as the altar in Paston Church

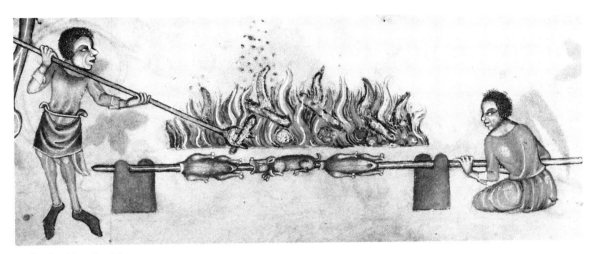

7.1b. Cooking food for the household

vital link between the local community and central government acting, for example, as members of parliament and as justices of the peace, administering the king's law, or co-operating in the collection of his taxes. Indeed, these medieval gentlemen–landowners were a very important group in the political world of the fifteenth century. But behind the world of politics lay a private world very similar to our own, driven by snobbery and social climbing, obsessed with property and money, concerned with marriage, love and the happiness of the family. Their values dominated political and private life for the next three centuries, and in the history of the Paston family of Norfolk, we can see something of the way in which this distinctive identity emerged.

The Pastons stand out among the massed gentryfolk of fifteenth century England because their voluminous family correspondence has survived to the present day – over a thousand letters, together with copies of wills, inventories of household goods, petitions and tradesmen's bills, exchanged between members of the family and their servants between 1425 and 1510. The letters are not unique; we have similar, but much smaller, fifteenth century collections belonging to the Stonor family in Oxfordshire[4] and to the merchant family of Cely based in London and Bristol,[5] but the Paston letters are the richest and most extensive source. They include a far higher proportion of letters written by and to women, and what they have to tell us ranges from the details of domestic arrangements – as when Margery Paston (writing to her husband in London in 1451) asks: 'that you will vouchsafe to send me another sugar loaf for my old is done. And also that ye well do make a girdle for your daughter, for she hath need thereof'[6] – to matters of high politics. William Paston wrote to his brother John in Norfolk after Edward IV's victory at Towton on 29

March, 1461: 'Our Sovereign Lord has won the field and upon Monday next after Palm Sunday was received into York with great solemnity and processions . . . King Henry, the Queen, the prince, the Duke of Somerset, the Duke of Exeter, Lord Roos, been fled into Scotland'.[7]

Like many of their contemporaries, the Pastons were among the *nouveaux riches* of the fifteenth century, who had pushed their way up the social ladder in the years following the Black Death, which struck England in the mid-fourteenth century. In three generations, the Pastons rose from serfdom to gentility, respectable enough to furnish members of parliament and royal judges. This remarkable tale of social mobility gives a very good idea of the calibre of the people who were now gathering local power in England into their hands.

During the lifetime of John Paston, an unfriendly contemporary from his own village wrote a somewhat scathing history of the family.[8] Clement Paston was a 'good plain husbandman' who had five or six score acres at Paston, much of it bond land, and a 'little poor watermill'. Clement Paston rode bareback on his horse – he could not afford a saddle – carrying his grain to be ground and he had no manors or income from rents. But he married judiciously, to Beatrix Somerton, a bond woman whose brother was already beginning to make his way up the social ladder on the fringes of the legal world, acting as an attorney and seller of ecclesiastical pardons, like the

7.3. The ruins of Somerton Church

unattractive pardoner of Chaucer's *Canterbury Tales*. Geoffrey Somerton 'gathered many pence and half-pence and therewith made a fair chapel' in his own village. Geoffrey's chapel is now an evocative ruin, but its scale suggests the lucrative nature of his chosen profession. Clement and Beatrix Paston had a son, William, whom they sent to school, even borrowing money to do so. With some help from Uncle Geoffrey, the attorney, William made his way to London and there learnt the law. He was rapidly successful, and was soon paid fees by the mayor and bishop of Norwich, and by the prior of Bromholm to look after their interests in London. By 1429, when he was fifty years old, he was made a judge, the crown to his meteoric career. It was his son John who was buried in Bromholm priory.

This rise from bondman to royal judge is mirrored in the remarkable growth of the Paston family estates. The grandfather Clement, who died in 1419, had no manors but simply farmed a

7.4. Letter to John Paston with the word 'churles' cut out

hundred or so acres in Paston. His grandson John's land stretched across three counties and included a great castle at Caister, several manor houses in Norfolk, and a town house in Norwich itself.

Like any *arrivistes*, the Pastons were sensitive about their origins and were subjected to unfriendly neighbourhood taunts.[9] In 1448, a brawl broke out on a Sunday morning at Gresham where the judge's widow Agnes and her daughter-in-law Margaret, were staying. John Wymondham, an old enemy of the Pastons, and James Gloys, the Paston family chaplain, fell into a slanging match in the street, while mass was being sung in the church. The noise was such that the two women rushed out of the church during the service and, as Margaret wrote to her husband: 'I bade Gloys go into my mother's place again, and so he did. And then Wymondham called my mother and me strong whores and said the Pastons and all their kin were churles [bondmen] of Gemingham and we said he lied, knave and churle as he was.'[10] The interesting thing to note about this letter, is that it has been deliberately mutilated. The word 'churles' has been cut out, probably by John Paston when he received the letter in London, for fear that the accusation might fall into unfriendly hands. It was not only that the Pastons were concerned about their social standing; these accusations of servile status also threatened their status as landowners. If the Pastons were serfs, then their rivals could argue that they were not entitled to hold land as freemen. Indeed, Lord Scales claimed Paston land in 1465 on exactly these grounds, saying that 'Johannes Paston armiger esset nativus dicti Regis', that is, John Paston Esquire should be a serf of the said King.[11] But in the next year, 1466, Edward IV and his council were persuaded of the distinction of the Paston lineage (encouraged perhaps by financial inducements) and issued a warrant declaring that the Pastons were 'gentlemen descended lineally of worshipful blood since the conquest' when their first ancestor, one Wulstan had come out of France with his kinsman Sir William Glanville, the founder of Bromholm priory at Paston.[12] The rise of the Paston family now had the seal of royal approval.

Much of the success of the Paston family depended on judicious marriages. Medieval marriage was not just a cornerstone of private happiness but also the key to public prosperity. The choice of a wife was one of the most important decisions a fifteenth century gentleman could make – or have made for him.

First and foremost, wives brought lands and money to their husbands, and marriage proposals were frequently discussed in the most cold-blooded terms. John Paston III[13] wrote in these terms to his mother in 1478 when he was in London:

7.5. The entrance to
Bromholm Priory

Also mother, I heard while I was in London where there was a
goodly young woman to marry, who was daughter to one Seff, a
mercer, and she shall have £200 pounds in money to her marriage
[her dowry] and 20 marks per annum from land after the decease of
a stepmother of hers who is upon fifty years of age . . . I spoke with
some of the maid's friends and have got their good wills to have her
married to my brother Edmund.[14]

What mattered was the dowry and the expected annual income, after
the death of a fifty-year-old stepmother, which this nameless daughter
of a London mercer would bring to the Paston estate.

But after marriage these women could come to play a very active
role in the managing of the family fortunes. Husbands were often
absent on business for long periods, and the day-to-day running of the
family estates fell to the women of the household. Beatrix, Agnes and
Margaret Paston had to maintain, guard and extend, where possible,

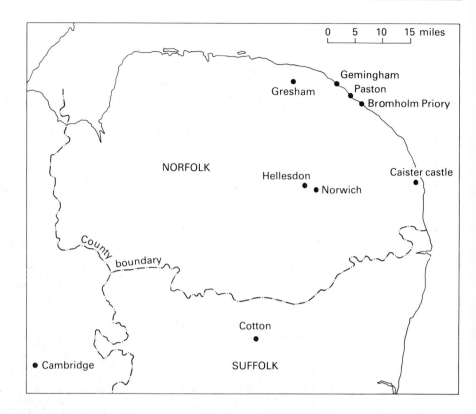

7.6. Places visted by Margaret Paston in 1465

the Paston interests in Norfolk while their husbands pursued the same ends in London. It could be dangerous: in January 1449 Lord Moleyns and his men drove Margaret Paston out of the manor house at Gresham and she had to retreat to Norwich.[15] Although Margaret might write to her husband as to what course of action she should take: 'I pray you send me word by the bringer of this, how you will that I be demened', in fact she had often to act on her own initiative because there were no instructions. In her husband's absence, Margaret carried his authority and in her 'demening' lay the maintenance of the Paston standing in the county. This involved frequent movement around different Paston manors, holding court, collecting rents, seeing to the upkeep of buildings and checking on the activities of the bailiffs, reeves and lesser servants. In 1465 Margaret's itinerary was strenuous (not least when we remember that she carried most of her household furnishings with her and that her home had to be made when she arrived). In April she was at Caister, in May at Hellesdon, June at Norwich, July back to Caister, August again at Hellesdon, then to Caister and back once more to Hellesdon, in September to London to visit her husband in the Fleet prison, then back to Cotton, to Norwich, then to Caister and then finally back to Norwich, presumably for Christmas.

7.7. A view of London in the early sixteenth century

However able their wives, however secure their standing in the countryside, these country gentlemen knew that fortunes were ultimately made and lost in the courts of Westminster. In London, country gentlemen could forge the links with powerful men that would safeguard their own prosperity and, perhaps, even secure the patronage of the king.

The efforts of the Pastons to secure the lion's share of the estates of Sir John Fastolf were typical. Fastolf left John Paston, in somewhat dubious circumstances, as virtually his sole executor. John seized his opportunity and claimed the jewel of the Fastolf estates, Caister Castle, although his claim did not go unchallenged either locally in Norfolk or in the king's courts. In the end, it was the gallant and wayward Sir John Paston, his eldest son, who, by attaching himself to the court of Edward IV, managed to persuade the king to confirm the Paston title to Caister and other Fastolf properties. It took nearly twenty years of unremitting effort.[16]

While in London, the Paston men led a very different life from that which they enjoyed in the domestic circle in Norfolk. Sir John sometimes travelled with the royal household, but he and the other Pastons usually stayed at inns when they came to London, for the family did not own a London town house. Only great nobles like the Duke of York or the Bishop of Ely would have undertaken the expense of a London house. Sir John had a semi-permanent arrangement with the proprietress at the George on Paul's Wharf on the Thames below the cathedral: she took letters and messages and provided a home from home for him, although Sir John once wrote to his mother, 'I found my chamber and shift not so clean as I desired'.[17] The growth of the hostelry trade in London was a marked feature of the fifteenth century when travel became more common and decent lodging in the city a necessity. The letters between the two brothers, Sir John II and John III, are full of references to London ladies, many of whom, but not all, were sought in marriage. The love-life of Sir John in particular was fraught. He was a chivalrous man and the role of the idealised, inaccessible lady in his life was played by Elizabeth, Duchess of Norfolk: 'I think my lady shall have my service above any lady earthly.'[18] His more earthly ladies included 'the mayde at the Bull in Westminster' who sent him a gold ring as a token, Mistress Elizabeth Higgins and her daughter at the Black Swan and Gretkyn and Babekyn in Calais, among many others.[19] John became engaged in 1469 to Mistress Anne Haute, a near kinswoman of Lord Scales and a cousin of Queen Elizabeth Woodville, perhaps as a means of forwarding his claims to Caister. But within two years both parties appear to have tried to break the engagement in spite of his mother Margaret's warning: 'And afore God, ye are as greatly bound to her as if you were married: and therefore I charge you upon my blessing that ye be as true to her as if she were married to you in all respects.'[20] It was not however until 1477 that the necessary papal dispensation came from Rome.

This had been a costly mistake but John began at once to look around for a bride. His mother counselled him to marry a woman whom he could love 'so that she be such as ye can think to have issue by: or else by my troth I had rather ye never married in your life.'[21] In fact Sir John found a lady whom he could love and by whom he did have issue, a daughter Constance, although he had not married his mistress before he died. Despite this Margaret Paston remembered her eldest son's illegitimate daughter in her will and gave her 10 marks.[22]

This memorial is a touching reminder of the emotional ties that linked members of medieval landowning families. Despite the hard-headed practicality which dominated the marriage market, romance was often present. Courtship and romantic love, however, tended to follow the marriage agreement, not precede it. Margaret Paston wrote to her husband in London a year after their marriage when she was expecting their first child:

> I pray that ye will wear the ring with the image of St Margaret that I sent you for a remembrance till you come home. You have left me such a remembrance that maketh me to think upon you both day and night when I would sleep.

Even after nearly twenty years of marriage she could write in 1459:

> I am sorry that ye shall not be home for Christmas. I pray ye that you will come as soon you may. I shall think myself half a widow because you shall not be at home.[23]

Margaret's daughter-in-law, Margery, who married her son John III in 1447, wrote him letters in the February before their marriage addressed to 'Right worshipful and well beloved valentine'. Margery's father was striking a hard bargain and was not prepared to offer more than a hundred pounds dowry with his daughter. Margery acknowledged that this was far less than John had hoped for but, she urged, 'if you could be content with that good, and my poor person, I would be the merriest maiden on ground'. One or other of the men relented for the couple were married and four years later Margery wrote a postscript to a letter to her husband when he was away on business in London: 'Sir, I pray you if ye tarry long at London that it will please you to send for me, for I think long since I lay in your arms'.[24]

In the absence of their husbands, the Paston women had a host of servants with whom their relationships were of great importance to the success of the family. There was the family chaplain, James Gloys; the bailiff, Richard Calle; James Gresham who worked for three generations of Pastons; William Lomnour, who acted as a family friend and agent on their behalf; and John Pampyng and Thomas Playter, who acted as clerks and wrote many of the letters, as well as serving as trusted retainers. All of these men were variously described as gentlemen or esquires; some were distant relatives and all held positions of trust. Another servant, John Daubenay, died in the Paston fight to hold Caister Castle; Richard Calle actually married Margery, the daughter of John and Margaret Paston, and the widow of William Lomnour married Edmund Paston as his second wife. The other Paston daughter, Anne, became amorously entangled with John Pampyng but did not marry him. These gentlemen–servants were the friends and allies of their employers, their trusted companions who wrote intimate letters for them and executed delicate and crucial commissions. They were expected to remain with the family through

7.8. A landed gentleman at home with his servants

thick and thin and, in return, the good master was obliged 'not to put servants from him like masterless hounds'.[25]

In many ways the Pastons seem to have been closer to their servants than to their children. This is not surprising for, while the servants were almost continuously with their employers, the children were frequently sent away. A Venetian who visited England in the 1490s observed that an Englishman:

However rich he may be, sends his children away into the houses of others whilst he, in return, receives those of strangers into his own. And on inquiring the reason for this severity they answered that they did it in order that their children might learn better manners. But I, for my part, believe that they do it because they like to enjoy all their comforts themselves, and that they are better served by strangers than they would be by their own children.[26]

There is certainly a toughness in the attitude of the Pastons towards their children and this harshness is particularly apparent in the women (who perhaps had more to do with the children). Elizabeth Paston, the judge's daughter, was still unmarried at his death and her mother Agnes refused to allow her to speak with any man, whether visitor or servant, and beat her sometimes twice a day – 'her head broken in two or three places'. What provoked this maltreatment on the part of her mother is difficult now to grasp.[27] In fact Elizabeth did not marry until she was thirty and was still bearing children well into her forties. But when Margery Paston took it into her head to become engaged to the family bailiff, Richard Calle, the whole family joined ranks against her. Calle was a good servant but he was a servant and, however educated and prosperous he might be, he was not of 'worshipful blood'. In spite of all their efforts, the Pastons could not challenge the validity of the vows that Calle and Margery had exchanged. Sadly Margaret wrote to her son, Margery's brother, 'Remember you, as I do, that we have lost in her but a brethele [a lightweight thing] and set it the less to heart . . . for were he [Calle] dead at this hour she should never be at mine heart as she was.'[28] Since we have so little correspondence exchanged between the women members of the Paston family it is hard to know how close they were to each other's hearts. But it is clear that John II, despite his extravagance and waywardness, was cherished by his mother who frequently urged his case with his father.

His brother wrote to John in London in 1475:

My mother sendeth you God's blessing and hers, and she would fain have you at home with her; and if you be once met she telleth me ye shall not lightly depart till death depart you.[29]

In fact, John died not long after this letter was written, unmarried and alone. He has written to his mother that he intended to leave the busy world of the royal court 'and come home to you and be your husband and bailiff'.[30] But it was not to be. In that phrase, however, we catch again a glimpse not only of that close inter-relationship between family and servants, but also of the genuine affection which bound together the members of these gentry families.

The decision of the Pastons to send their children away from home was not arbitrary and irrational. Education, above all in the law, was crucial to a gentleman's prosperity, and a woman would be much more attractive to prospective husbands if she had learnt the social graces of 'people of worship' in a gentle household. Perhaps because of their own recent rise into the gentry class, the Pastons were particularly conscious of the need to educate and train their children. Judge William Paston, whose father had borrowed money to send him to school, took trouble to see that his children were, in their turn, educated. Three of his four sons spent time at Cambridge University and the fourth, Edmund, studied in London at Clifford's Inn. John Paston, the judge's eldest son and heir, spent time at Trinity Hall and Peterhouse in Cambridge as well as at the Inner Temple in London, where it was reported 'there been many which sore desire your presence'. Perhaps John felt himself to be over-educated for, of his five

7.9. The Paston family tree

7.10. A page from
Lydgate's *Siege of
Thebes*

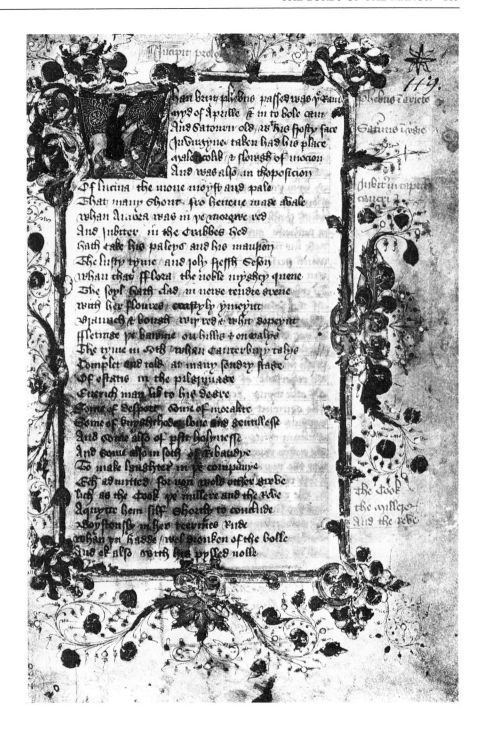

sons, only one, Walter, went to university – in this case Oriel College,
Oxford – although the two Johns were reported by their uncle in
London to be learning 'right well' and William, the youngest, was sent

to Eton where he reported 'I lack nothing but versifying which I trust to have with a little continuance'.[31]

The evidence of the letters themselves shows that all the Paston men could write although they often employed scribes. Their hands varied greatly and the crudest hand was that of John I – who had studied both at Cambridge and at an Inn of Court – and the most accomplished was that of his son, Sir John II, who had officially studied in neither place. The Paston women, however, could barely write and always employed scribes although Margery subscribed letters written by her secretary after her marriage 'by your servant and bedeswoman Margery Paston' in a distinctively halting and uncontrolled hand, 'as of someone beginning to learn to write'.[32] But even though the women could not write much, if at all, they may have been able to read. When she was about seventeen, Anne Paston owned a book containing Lydgate's poem on the *Siege of Thebes*.[33] There are references to books, especially textbooks, passing between the Paston menfolk, but it was Sir John Paston II who seemed to have been the greatest reader and collector. He employed a scribe, William Ebesham, to copy books for him, chivalrous treatises in French, and a 'little book of Physic' amongst other labours.[34] He was anxious about the books that had belonged to Sir John Fastolf 'in French, Latin and English' which might have been lost at the siege of Caister Castle, and he was extremely keen to acquire the library which belonged to the family chaplain, James Gloys. However, he admitted that since he could not pay for the books, he would pray instead for his soul.[35] Not long before his death, John drew up in his own hand an inventory of his English books, seventeen in all, which included works on heraldry, and chivalrous tales about the *Death of Arthur, La Belle Dame sans Merci* and *Sir Gawain and the Green Knight*. He even owned a copy of *The Game and Play of Chesse* 'in preente' which had indeed been printed by William Caxton only a couple of years before.[36] The alacrity with which country gentlemen caught on to the new fashion of printed books, especially in English, demonstrates how these landowners were beginning to shape a distinctive intellectual world of their own. A world which, while rooted in the mundane lawsuits and estate management of their own day, yet looked back to the chivalrous exploits described by Sir Thomas Malory in the *Morte D'Arthur* or by Froissart in his chronicles of the early battles of the Hundred Years War with France.

For much of the middle ages, the church had controlled men's intellectual horizons through a hierarchy of parish priests, cloistered monks and preaching friars. But the gentlefolk of the fifteenth century used education quite differently – for the practical purposes of law and estate management, and for the enjoyment of historical tales and

7.11. An inventory of John Paston's books

romances. Families like the Pastons were representative of this new literate, nationalistic and above all secular culture that had the potential to upset the established balance between church and state which had for so long regulated the medieval world. Just as Clement Paston had seized the opportunities presented by population dearth after the Black Death, so the Pastons of the sixteenth century would seize the chance to buy up monastic land which had been forfeited to the crown. The king and his subjects both made the most of their opportunities: a new Britain was in the making.

Further Reading

R. Barber (ed.), *The Pastons: a Family in the Wars of the Roses* (Harmondsworth, 1984); N. Davis (ed.), *Paston Letters and Papers of the Fifteenth Century*, 2 vols (Oxford, 1971 and 1976); A. Hanham (ed.), *The Cely Letters, 1472–88* (Oxford, 1975); C.L. Kingsford (ed.), *Stonor Letters and Papers 1290–1483*, 2 vols (Camden Society, 1919).

Towns and Trade

Richard Mackenney

The society of medieval Britain was essentially 'feudal' in character. That is to say, it was divided into three basic groups, each defined by a specific function: those who prayed; those who fought; those who worked. Those who prayed, the clergy, gave spiritual and moral guidance and imposed at least some restraint on the violent habits of those who fought, the knights. The position of this group as defenders of Christendom entitled them to a living at the expense of those who worked, the peasantry, from whom feudal lords exacted or extorted goods and services.[1]

The structure was a rigid one. It was difficult to become a priest without a set of profound and solemn undertakings and knighthood became a status to which, increasingly, a 'seigneur' was born, not one to which he was or could be elevated. The exploitations of ecclesiastical and secular lords meant that for the peasant, the possibilities of social or even geographical mobility were very limited. The groups then were tightly defined: hard to enter, hard to abandon and virtually impossible to combine with any other function than the one which the 'group label' designated.

Yet, by the end of the fourteenth century we find in the prologue to Chaucer's *Canterbury Tales*, a list of characters which surely stems from a more diverse and variegated society. True, there are a knight and a number of clergymen, but there are also a haberdasher, a carpenter, a weaver and a dyer. There is even someone who made a living as a servant to one of the Inns of Court, a maunciple, and inns of another sort provide the setting in which the tales are told.[2]

What had generated the new diversity? Not all Chaucer's characters are townsmen, by any means, but it is undoubtedly the case that the towns were one of the key agencies of social change in medieval Britain. Medieval towns were very different from the urban commu-

8.1. Chaucer's pilgrims

nities of our own day. We tend to think of towns in the twentieth century as very densely populated areas with the majority of the inhabitants engaged in commerce or industry or both. But modern cities are the products of the industrial revolution and their sheer scale makes them very different from their medieval forebears.

The entire population of Britain in about 1300 was probably around 5 million – only half the size of modern London alone. Few towns anywhere in Europe had a population of even a hundred thousand people – Venice and Florence maybe, Naples and Paris perhaps. But there was nothing on this scale in Britain which, like the rest of Europe outside northern Italy, southern Germany and Flanders, remained overwhelmingly rural in character. Nine people out of every ten lived in the countryside. How could towns come into being – let alone survive – in an economy based on agriculture and a society whose life revolved around the village? What was important in this regard was not the number of towns or the number of their inhabitants, but the kind of life style that became possible within them and the possibilities they opened up for Britain's future development.

Nevertheless, towns were as much the products of the rural world as they were a departure from it. In terms of types of work and way of life, towns were quite different from the feudal countryside. But it was also the case that the towns depended on the human and material resources of the countryside in order to grow. The strange relationship of conflict and harmony is the main theme of this chapter, which is built around four related questions.

The first concerns population. What caused medieval people to settle in communities which might come to be called towns? And secondly, when such communities had formed, what did the inhabitants do to make a living? Third is the question of legal status – a seemingly narrow and technical point but crucial to our theme. What guarantees were offered by a suspicious, even hostile, feudal world to ensure the continued existence of towns? Finally comes the problem of characterising urban society. Given their economic life and legal safeguards, did town-dwellers form societies with their own distinctive features?

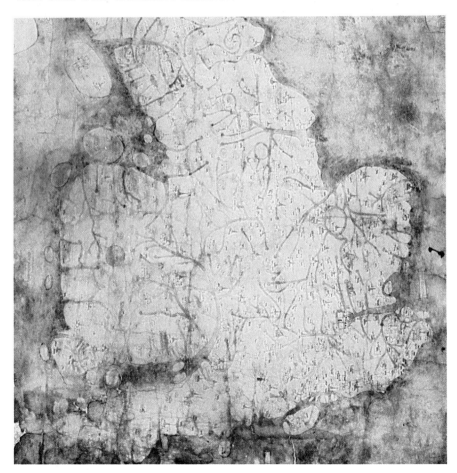

8.2. The Gough Map, showing England's towns in the fourteenth century

Quoniam in dominus dim
super omnem terram : nimis
tus es super omnes deos

8.3. Taking the harvest to market

Our first task is to look at the people who lived in towns and what took them there. This sounds straightforward enough, but there are serious problems concerning our evidence – or the lack of it. Historians of medieval Britain are fortunate in having rich archival resources – both in London and elsewhere – which fill in all kinds of detail; on production and export, on the regulation of markets by guilds and the court cases which resulted from contraventions, on relations with the monarchy and so forth. But in terms of how large the towns were at any particular time, how many of them existed and how they grew, there is a scarcity of hard facts, and a lack of uniformity in the records. However, at least one generalisation is possible for almost any town of the pre-industrial era; the death rate was higher than the birth rate. The streets of modern towns are (generally) clean and paved. In the middle ages, towns were provided with only the most rudimentary public services and the inevitable result was squalor and disease. Conditions were worsened by the community's dependence – like the peasantry's – on the success of the harvest, and – unlike country-dwellers – on suppliers who would bring rural produce in carts or on their backs to sell at the town market or fair. As in parts of the world today, hunger and sickness walked hand in hand. Empty stomachs were more susceptible to disease and the insanitary conditions of the towns made the ravages of any epidemic all the more terrible. By the later middle ages, there were public latrines in London, Leicester, Southampton and Winchester and some water was piped. But before then overcrowding, the lack of running water and of sewerage made disease a constant hazard.[3] As a consequence, any absolute increase in the size of a town's population was dependent on immigration from the countryside. And this is what happened in the twelfth and thirteenth centuries before the Black Death ravaged the entire population in the later fourteenth century.[4]

Within this period of general expansion (1100–1340), the growth in the size and number of towns was marked. Stratford-upon-Avon provides an intriguing case history.[5] In the Domesday survey of 1086, Stratford was a manor which supported only 21 villeins – dramatically outnumbered by the one thousand eels which were supposed to swim in the waters of the estate. By about 1250, Stratford had become a thriving borough. Part of the manor had been divided into plots of land available from the landlord, the bishop of Worcester, in return for a fixed cash rent and without further obligations to the local lord. This had attracted 234 tenants and the total population of the borough may have been as high as a thousand. One or two of them had come from as far afield as Leicester and Birmingham – an odd thought considering the relative sizes of the three towns today. However, very few of the immigrants came from more than 16 miles away, a neat illustration of the way in which a town could come into being as a concentrated form of local, rural society.

But what brought them together? This had a great deal to do with

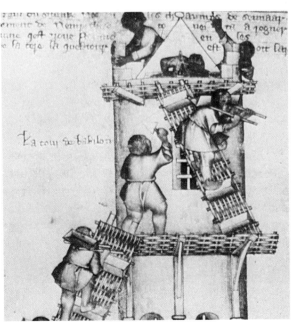

8.4. English builders at work

what people in towns did to earn a living. In many cases, in the aftermath of the Norman Conquest, the regrouping of the population into an urban community was determined by the requirements of the ruling class. Many town-dwellers – including those who built churches and castles – were still *laboratores* who toiled to meet the needs of lords ecclesiastical and lay.

The great building projects of Norman bishops at Lincoln, York, Norwich and Winchester demanded relatively large numbers of craftsmen skilled in particular trades and they, as well as their noble employers, required the provision of services like food and shelter 'on site'. Much the same can probably be said of the castles built by Norman lords – like those at Warwick or Colchester. The latter was built on the foundations of the Anglo-Saxon burgh and a still older fortified site.[6] And some Scottish burghs, like Roxburgh or Edinburgh, grew up on fortified positions.[7]

The population of the new centres might expand at different times of the year, and short-term visitors – pilgrims to Canterbury for instance – would set up a new chain of demand to be met by local suppliers. By the time visitors began to travel regularly to Becket's shrine, towns had begun to develop in a different way. Their new character gave them a new role in British life and a more forceful one. In the course of the twelfth century, and certainly by the year 1200, urban developments marked a shift away from the world of cathedrals and castles and in the long term a challenge to it.

The mainspring of this development was the growth of trade. Here

8.5. Scene from the Luttrell Psalter

again we are using a word which in a medieval context has connotations very different from those it has today. The international commerce which we take for granted was significant in medieval Britain not for its size but for its very existence. Trade with other countries was handled by relatively few towns. Southampton and London had important links with northern France, with Flanders and with Italy. Particularly significant in the life of these two ports were the wool exports for which England was so celebrated. Bristol on the other hand began to develop its trade to supply England with the products of the Angevin kings' possessions in western France. From Gascony the merchants of Bristol brought salt and wine – though whether the former stimulated demand for the latter is unclear.[8]

Within English medieval towns, however, trade was often controlled by the more advanced business techniques and superior organisation of foreign merchants. Today, London's banks are concentrated in

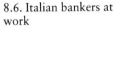

8.6. Italian bankers at work

Lombard Street which betrays the fact that financial dealings in the medieval city were dominated by Italians. It was the Bardi and the Peruzzi of Florence who financed Edward III's early campaigns in the Hundred Years War. Many commercial exchanges were handled by merchants at the Steelyard, the home of Germans from the league of towns called the Hanse which dominated the Baltic trade in timber, tallow, and furs. Similar communities of Hansards operated in the north at Hull and at York.[9]

England's exports were again the products of the countryside, not the manufactures of the towns. Of these, far and away the most important was wool. By the end of the thirteenth century, there were almost certainly more sheep than people in Britain. It must have taken around six million animals to supply the 30,000 sacks which left England every year in the 1290s.[10] The importance of the wool trade is still recorded in British life, for the Lord Chancellor sits on the Woolsack, a sack containing what was once England's most important product and which, for much of the thirteenth and fourteenth centuries, gave work to looms from Flanders to Florence.

Of much less importance in Britain's overseas trade were the hides of animals and the tin which came from the stannaries of Devon and Cornwall, both products serving to emphasise the rural basis of urban commerce in the middle ages.[11] Even when, in the thirteenth century, the English began to produce cloth rather than wool for export, much of it was processed in rural communities where a stage of the complicated manufacture might provide an occupation in lives generally dominated by work on the land. The 'domestic system' of production with spinning and even weaving being carried on in the home was just as practicable, and just as significant, in the countryside as in the towns. Indeed, some processes (such as fulling) could be more easily carried on in rural areas where a water mill might be more accessible.[12]

Like manufacture, trade too was a largely local phenomenon and commerce was based on the products of the countryside. Markets drew people to towns and seem to have kept some of them there. Stratford's earliest known inhabitants tended to come from villages about six miles away – the approximate distance a man might walk to market and back in a day. To serve the needs of the market town, there developed shops, stalls and areas where cloth might be dyed. The availability of food and shelter enabled artisans to concentrate on specialist occupations. This emerges from the remarkably detailed survey written for Bishop Walter de Cantelupe, lord of Stratford, in 1251–2. From this we can see that in the mid-thirteenth century, the borough had its shoemaker, weaver, fuller and dyer and a glover. The building trades provided work for smiths and carpenters while a

8.7. Rural workers carding and spinning wool, as well as working on the land

woman called Alice made a living as a ropemaker. The vitality of the town's economy is reflected in the fact that the medieval market centre has helped to shape the modern town. The streets which came into being in the thirteenth century, the formative period in Stratford's growth, still survive today. Bridge Street, High Street, Healey Street, Greenhill Street and Sheep Street all date back to the 1200s.

All the same, such expansion and development were not purely spontaneous. The feudal structure of society was by no means flexible. Within it developed these centres of bustle and movement where money, not birth or calling, determined a man's standing. But the towns needed to receive formal recognition of their right to exist from the lordly powers which surrounded them. This recognition took the form of a special legal status. The right to hold a market had to be acknowledged by the local lord. As if to show that even feudal society recognised the immense new possibilities which trade was opening up, lords began actively to promote the development of markets and towns.

The borough of Stratford was founded as an entity distinct from the

8.8. Site of the Norman castle and cathedral at Old Sarum

manor by the local lord, the bishop of Worcester, in 1196. He it was who set aside part of the manor and divided it into plots which he rented out for cash, not services. Other burdens of the manorial economy, such as the lord's right to exact tolls, were also lifted and it was the loosening of the bonds which tied men to their lords in personal obligation which gave the borough its essential features, its recognisable identity in a feudal world. This is not to say that the manor was eclipsed altogether. Far from it. The bishop of Worcester's manor at Stratford grew from 21 tenants in 1196 to 70 in the mid-thirteenth century. But it became known as 'Old Stratford' as distinct from the flourishing borough with its population of a thousand souls.

The same development occurred from Chipping Camden to Leeds. One of the most startling shifts in the organisation of social and economic life is provided by the experience of Salisbury. The modern cathedral town is a striking example of the sudden imposition of a new identity by the local lord. In the early thirteenth century, Bishop Poore moved his cathedral and residence away from its site at what we know as Old Sarum and founded a market in Salisbury itself. The bishop's move from a windy hill in the shadow of a castle to the more sheltered and accessible site of a market might symbolise the way in which urban life found its place in a feudal world.[13]

England's chief feudal lord, the king himself, was not slow to recognise the profitable possibilities of granting legal status in return for a money payment. By the time of King John, the crown itself had granted some hundred charters recognising the kind of rights enjoyed by the residents of Stratford and in about another two hundred cases, private lords had done the same. By the late thirteenth century, England alone may have had as many as 3,000 weekly markets, for this number of grants had been purchased from the crown.[14]

Inevitably, the old society and the new sometimes grated on each other and lords were reluctant to lose their traditional rights. In 1223, Alan Basset tried to reassert feudal power over the town of Buckingham, which had won its privileges within the manorial lands of the crown. King John had granted the manor to Basset. The new lord attempted to restrict the liberties of the town's merchants who, naturally enough, resisted the infringement of their freedoms which the lord's tolls embodied. It is an interesting footnote to the clash of two models of society that when the merchants took the case to law, they offered to have it settled either by jury or through trial by combat. They were prepared to take on the feudal world on its own terms.[15] But on the whole, the financial attractions of the towns made the lords acknowledge their existence through grants of privileges in return for cash. From the acknowledgement derived a vital idea: that the towns could offer their inhabitants personal freedom – and protect it.

London's citizens may have been exceptional in declaring in 1193 that they would have no king but their mayor. After all, Richard I was in captivity abroad and his brother and the nobles had already acknowledged that the city was a commune, subject to no external authority but the king's.[16] The case of William of Amesbury in 1237 is a more modest assertion of a similar principle – and perhaps it produced more concrete results. William had been a serf without personal freedom but had absconded from his master, Everard le Tyeis. The bailiffs of Andover protected him from the lord's efforts to return him to bondage on the grounds that William was a travelling merchant who had married a woman of the town. For this reason, they refused to deliver him to his lord and the outcome was that Everard gave up his claim to his former bondman, acknowledging William's freedom along with 'his whole brood'.[17]

Town air was freer and this was reflected in the structure of the society which breathed it. Freedom from seigneurial interference also meant freedom of association with others and this tended to produce the kind of solidarity expressed by the bailiffs of Andover with William of Amesbury. In the feudal world, loyalties were organised vertically, from man to lord. The townsman's loyalties were to his

8.9. Tavern scene

equals – to those of the same town, and within the town to those of the same trade or the same parish.

The most obvious and most enduring institutional expression of this was the guild, which extended the corporative principle into every walk of urban life – economic, social, political and religious. These institutions existed to regulate trade, to offer some support in the event of a member's illness, and consolation for his widow and orphans in the event of his death. Of course, this did not mean that all guildsmen were equal. Many of the guilds governed crafts which were organised around the strictly defined status of apprentice, journeyman and master and there were wide differences in the wealth and influence of different corporations.[18]

There were important social distinctions within the towns. At the top of the hierarchy we find the merchants, often retailers as well as wholesalers. Their guilds, such as the one at Buckingham which

8.10. Merchant Adventurers' Hall, York: the Great Hall

resisted the claims of Alan Basset, gave the early borough its identity. Some of them may also have been the officials of lords who saw the opportunity for advancement in the town – such at least is the background of the mayors of thirteenth century Lincoln.[19]

These merchant interests developed into an urban aristocracy, a patriciate, which dominated city office and which regulated urban trade. The meeting places of mercers, goldsmiths, and cutlers are still prominent in the landscape of central London. The deliberations of their members – who will have included people like Dick Whittington and William Caxton – gave shape and character to town life.[20] The guildhalls in which they met were often near the market places they supervised, and the hall of the Merchant Adventurers at York seems to embody the exuberance of their economic activities and the solidarity of their social position.[21]

Below the merchants, and often in conflict with them, were associations of craftsmen. They too formed guilds and sought to regulate the standard of manufactures: buildings, clothing, household wares and the proper measures of food, thus meeting the needs of an expanding and more complicated urban society. Their monopolies served to maintain the standards of production and to ease the regulation of markets. They helped to standardise weights and measures and to punish offenders like the fishmonger whose wares were not fresh and the baker who sold short. In Shrewsbury, weavers who contravened their ordinances could be fined – the money being shared among bailiffs, commonalty and guild. In return for guarantees of quality control and consumer protection, the borough granted the craft a monopoly which protected local guilds in local markets against external competition.[22] The more noxious trades were forbidden to practise in the towns themselves. Kilnmen and tanners were usually confined to the suburbs which formed outside the town gates, while in Southampton blacksmiths were banned from the High Street in the fourteenth century, presumably because their forges were a fire hazard.[23]

Relations between 'guilds merchant' and the crafts were often tense and turbulent. The two types of guild were constantly in competition and the desire to dominate often clashed with the desire to climb. In thirteenth century London, there was a series of such conflicts – lorimers against saddlers, cutlers against chaplers. The fiercest disputes were often in the textile trades. In 1300, an attempt was made to deny the weavers the franchise and their legal rights in cases involving burgesses – amongst whom, of course, one would find the drapers and dyers who gave the weavers their employment. In 1336, mercantile interests in the city's government even abolished the guild's monopoly of weaving.[24]

But not all of urban life was contained within the walls of guildhall or workshop. Many, certainly by the fourteenth century, made a living as hawkers and hucksters who operated independent of associations, plying their wares from one town to another;[25] and there were other members of urban society who found no security in group identity. The Jews of medieval York were massacred in 1190 in one of Europe's first outbursts of anti-semitic hatred. Their lot was never easy. Nor was that of the poor: lepers, beggars, cripples, widows and orphans whose misery was divinely sanctioned and assured of reward in the hereafter. They were poor whether times were good or bad. When times grew consistently bad in the late fourteenth century, there were some measures to provide greater material support in the towns. Great charitable bequests had made possible the building of hospitals like St Leonard's at York as early as 1135 while from the chantry chapels built to commemorate the wealthy in Bristol, the poor might expect the occasional dole.[26]

All the same, guilds were more interested in supporting members than outsiders and their introversion helped to produce a certain atrophy in urban society by the later fifteenth century. A mastery was, after all, a 'mystery' and guilds existed to protect the secrets of a trade, to provide conviviality for the living and commemoration of the dead. This latter function could indeed supersede all others in guild life for not all guilds were connected with economics and politics. Many brotherhoods of laymen honeycombed the medieval town. These confraternities existed for devotional purposes: to bear candles in procession on feast days, perhaps to maintain an altar at one of the town's churches, to provide some succour – spiritual rather than material – to the urban poor. The guilds of York were particularly famous for their processions in honour of the Blessed Sacrament. The guild of Corpus Christi was founded in 1408 and its membership included a duke of Gloucester who later became King Richard III. Perhaps he had contributed to the funding of the guilds' hospital of St Thomas of Canterbury, established in York in 1478.[27]

In York or Coventry, the guilds performed another function, this time in the cultural sphere. The great mystery plays of the fifteenth century which reminded society of sin, hell and damnation were put on by the city's corporations. Much of the self-consciously penitential devotion of late medieval guilds was stimulated by the prickings of conscience felt by money-makers after the Black Death. This, perhaps the greatest catastrophe Europe has ever seen, probably carried off a third of Britain's population and its effects are likely to have been all the more terrifying in the overcrowded towns.[28] To many, the recurrent plagues of the late fourteenth and fifteenth centuries looked like God's punishment on a sinful world.

However, the late fourteenth century also produced the poets Langland and Chaucer whose writings reveal a more advanced society, more diverse if more scarcely populated, and in many ways more civilised. In the great period of growth from about 1100 to about 1340 and in the period of adaptation and adjustment after the Black Death, towns had added a new and dynamic diversity to British society and were to play a crucial part in the new era of expansion and opportunity which opened at the end of the fifteenth century.

In this new age, most towns expanded, but the growth of London was nothing short of phenomenal. After about 1500, as Chaucer's pilgrims dissolved into Shakespeare's characters, the capital began to exert an extraordinary pull on the rest of Britain. London was by now becoming one of Europe's great metropolitan centres and beginning to exercise the kind of economic and cultural dominance which we still see today.

Further Reading

G.W.S. Barrow, *Feudal Britain* (London, 1971); J. Harvey, *Medieval Craftsmen* (London, 1975); C. Platt, *The English Medieval Town* (London, 1979); M.M. Postan, *The Medieval Economy and Society* (London, 1972); G.A. Williams, *Medieval London: from Commune to Capital* (London, 1963).

CHAPTER NINE

The Church and the Love of Christ

David Carpenter

In 1199, John, the new king of England, and his bishop of Lincoln, Hugh of Avalon, visited together the tombs of Henry II and Richard I at the monastery of Fontevrault in Anjou. Before entering the church, they paused beneath the great sculpture above the west doorway. It depicted Christ, sitting in judgement. On Christ's left, those, including kings, who had led sinful lives were being dragged off by devils to the torments of hell fire. On Christ's right, those who had followed his teachings were being conducted to heaven by smiling angels. Bishop Hugh, as a warning to the new king, pointed to the sculpture and urged John to heed its message. John replied at once that he fully intended to be amongst those admitted to the joys of paradise.[1]

The king's sentiments would have been shared by the great majority of people throughout Europe. For this was an age of faith. Apart from the Jews, there were few without at least a general belief in Christ and the realities of a Christian heaven and hell. The one established institution which was concerned to order people's lives in conformity with Christ's words, and thus secure for them salvation, was the catholic church, with its head the pope in Rome. Its task was awesome. On the one hand, it had to provide instruction and guidance for the great bulk of the population, a population which was largely ignorant of the precise teachings of Jesus and certainly unable to live up to them. On the other hand, it had to give opportunities and encouragement to the exceptional person, to the spiritual enthusiast, concerned to lead a Christ-like life, and dedicate himself completely to Christ's service.

How did the church measure up to this challenge? I shall consider first the chief area where it failed, for, despite great efforts it did fail in its general work of instruction and guidance at the vital grass-roots level of the parish, the level at which it came into most direct contact with the majority of the population. Secondly, I shall look at how the church succeeded in the twelfth and thirteenth centuries in providing opportunities for the spiritual enthusiast: succeeded by generating, outside the parochial framework, new religious orders, the Cistercian monks and the friars who witnessed in compelling fashion to the imitation and the love of Christ. Finally we shall see how the church of the later middle ages, the church that is of the fourteenth and fifteenth centuries, ceased to contain such elements of countervailing spirituality. The Cistercians and the friars declined. No new major orders were allowed to take their place and the spiritually-minded had now to find channels for their devotion outside the formal structure of the church. The ground was being prepared for John Wycliffe and the Lollards, for heresy, and ultimately for Reformation.

First let us look at the failure of the church at the level of the parish and its priest. The task of the priest was to take services in the church, and more generally to teach, by word and example, Christ's gospel. The great majority of his parishioners were likely to be illiterate, ignorant peasants. For them, what was needed was a very simple and basic statement of the essentials of a Christian life. According to his chaplain and biographer, Hugh of Avalon, bishop of Lincoln, for example, 'impressed on the minds of ordinary people that they must consider their vocation as summarised by the name Christian, and that they must be able to explain the meaning of this short and simple word to their friends. All sincere Christians must have chaste bodies, truthful tongues, and loving hearts – hearts, that is, full of love for God and for their neighbour. When at the last,' Hugh continued, 'the Lord shall judge every individual, he will not hold it against him that he has not been a hermit or a monk, but will reject him only if he has not been a real Christian'.[2] The kind of local priest required to put over this type of message, and even more difficult, to see that it was followed, was graphically described by Chaucer, in his Prologue to the *Canterbury Tales*. His 'poor parson' was indeed poor in material possessions, but he was rich in 'holy thought and work'. Chaucer's parson dwelt in his parish, and resisted the temptation to go off to London in search of preferment. Thunder and rain did not prevent him visiting sick parishioners, however remote their homes. He lived frugally, so that he had much to give to the poor. He was not contemptuous of the sinful, but had scant respect for the rich and powerful. Above all,

Christs lore and his apostles' twelve,
He taught – but first he followed it himselve.

Had the majority of parish priests been like Chaucer's, the situation of the church in the localities would have been good indeed. Unfortunately this was not the case. Large numbers of rectors, the men who actually received the revenues of the churches, neither lived nor worked within their parishes. The vicars and chaplains who were their deputies and assistants were frequently worldly, immoral and ignorant. When, in the 1190s, the holy man, Edmund of Eynsham, had a vision about the state of the church, it was largely concerned with the shocking situation in the parishes. Edmund was told:

> The daily acts of the rectors of churches and their assistants have deeply offended the Divine Majesty. Priests are polluted by every kind of sin, especially lechery. Everywhere churches are given to persons unfitted to rule them, whose depravity makes them hateful to God. They never think of the care of souls or of using the revenues of the church to assist the needy, but all the time they greedily strive to stuff their own money bags. The bad example of these rectors has contaminated and corrupted their flocks.

A hundred years later an inquiry into the state of nineteen parishes in part of Kent revealed that only one was wholly satisfactory. Six of the rectors were absentees; four were described as 'doing no good in the parish'. Most of the lower clergy, with day to day charge of the care of souls, were unfaithful to the vows of chastity. At the village of Hope All Saints, for example, the rector was away at university. William the chaplain, who ran the parish, was living with a woman. The Missal in the church was so dilapidated that services could hardly be taken. Nearby at St Martin's in Old Romney, the chaplain had to be suspended because of the state of the church. The chalice was broken and there were no service books at all.[3]

Could nothing be done to improve the situation in the parishes? Certainly valiant efforts were made. In the 1040s the papacy asserted its leadership of a great movement to reform the church. Popes presided over many councils which passed reforming legislation, for example in 1049 and 1074, and later in 1123, 1179 and 1215. Many of the decrees were concerned with the parish predicament. Those of 1215, for example, forbade pluralism, that is the holding of more than one church, and insisted that priests should serve their parishes personally, and not through deputies. The clergy were enjoined to avoid the sin of lust, to abstain from gluttony, drunkenness, dice and hunting, and to wear plain clothes.

The papacy was not content merely to promulgate reforming decrees. It also succeeded in committing churchmen to the task of implementing them. This was part and parcel of the process by which, in the eleventh and twelfth centuries, throughout Europe, the papacy turned a theoretical headship of the church into one which was highly practical. English ecclesiastics, for example, visited the pope with increasing frequency. Many attended the great reforming councils of 1179 and 1215. At the same time, the pope despatched a growing stream of decrees to England dealing with points of discipline and doctrine, and these, together with earlier papal pronouncements, were brought together in decretal collections and assiduously studied. Thus the papal programme of reform became widely known, and individual bishops struggled to implement it in their dioceses.[4] Hugh of Avalon, for example, as bishop of Lincoln between 1186 and 1200, made 'unflagging efforts to reform the lives of priests and clerks, and to restore all the churches of his diocese to their right condition'. A later bishop of Lincoln, Oliver Sutton (1280–99), made unceasing tours of inspection of the parishes throughout his diocese.[5]

The endeavours of bishops like Hugh and Oliver doubtless helped to secure individual priests like Chaucer's poor parson. But the sober records of tours of inspection, like that in Kent in the 1290s, show that the general state of the local clergy remained abysmally low. Why had the movement for reform failed? The answer to this question lies in the whole relationship between the church and ecclesiastical

9.1. Clerical misconduct

authority on the one hand, and the king and secular powers on the other. Throughout this period a large proportion of parish rectors were appointed by the lay lord of the local manor. This was because his ancestors had probably founded and endowed the church in the first place. (Even today, we can see how many churches are still next to the manor house.) In appointing the rector, the lord might take account of the spiritual needs of the parishioners. But very often he did not. His aim was simply to provide an income for a younger son or a clerk working in his service. Against men appointed by powerful and influential lords, it was almost impossible to enforce the legislation which forbade pluralism and required residence. Nor did such rectors give much thought to the suitability of their deputies for the care of souls. No wonder, therefore, that Edmund of Eynsham was told in his vision that 'everywhere churches are given to persons unfitted to rule them'.[6]

This problem over the appointment of parish priests was compounded by a similar one concerning the choice of bishops, a choice very often controlled by the king. In the twelfth and thirteenth centuries, there was a number of conscientious diocesan bishops. But such men were far from universal. All too often, the king secured the promotion of royal clerks and civil servants, who had little interest in reform and often continued their careers in the king's service after their elevation to the episcopal bench. Since it was up to the bishops to initiate improvements within the parishes, this situation made any concerted movement of reform impossible. Committed churchmen, of course, were well aware of the problem of lay control. The major purpose of the papal programme of reform in the eleventh century had been to free the church from the trammels of royal domination. But kings were bound to resist such an aim. They needed to regulate appointments both to reward royal clerks for faithful service, and to ensure that important centres of power, like bishoprics, were placed in safe and loyal hands. The Canterbury historian, Eadmer, remarked around 1110 that if a king ceased to control appointments, he would lose, in effect, 'half his kingdom'.[7]

Conflict between church and state was, therefore, inevitable. The climax in the European struggle came when Pope Gregory VII excommunicated and deposed the German emperor, Henry IV, and then forced him to stand for three days in the snow outside the castle of Canossa before allowing him in and granting him absolution. The eventual compromise in 1122 which settled the papal–imperial dispute, still left the emperor with a large degree of control over ecclesiastical appointments. It was the same in England. Here, the conflict had been settled in 1107 but broke out again in the dispute between Henry II and his archbishop of Canterbury Thomas Becket.

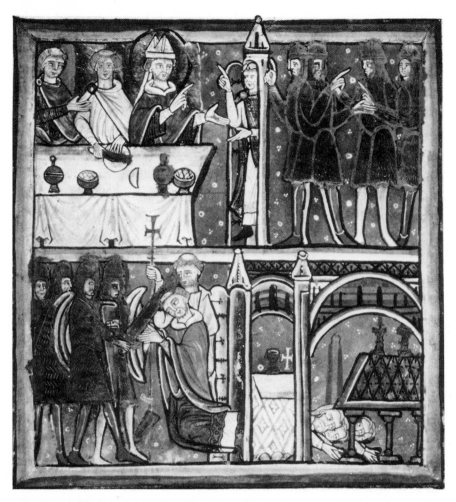

9.2. The murder of Thomas Becket

Becket was himself a political appointee, the king's most influential civil servant, whom Henry made archbishop in order to increase royal control over the church. When, instead, Becket stood up for ecclesiastical freedom, Henry's anger knew no bounds. His furious cry 'will no one rid me of this turbulent priest?' led to Becket's murder in his cathedral on 29 December 1170, with Henry's knights lopping off the top of the archbishop's head, a scene depicted in numerous medieval paintings and sculptures. To settle the crisis after the murder, Henry made concessions which facilitated the growth of papal authority over the church in England. But he retained substantial control over the area most vital to him – appointments. A form of free election by the church was allowed, but the reality was seen in Henry's order to the chapter at Winchester cathedral, 'I command you to hold a free election, but, nonetheless, I forbid you to elect anyone save Richard my clerk.' Thus, although on occasion Henry might welcome the choice of a bishop like Hugh of Avalon, he made quite sure that a high proportion of the bench was made up of royal clerks. Just such a man was Hubert Walter, appointed bishop of Salisbury by Richard I and later to be archbishop of Canterbury, who devoted himself to affairs of state as justiciar and chancellor of the realm. When Hugh of Avalon urged Hubert to abandon the business of state and apply himself to his archiepiscopal duties, he incurred only the archbishop's bitter enmity.[8]

The failure of reform meant, therefore, that in the typical medieval parish one would rarely find a parson capable of preaching Christ's gospel, by word or by example, to the great illiterate mass of the population. In the thirteenth century the words of Jesus were quoted, 'The blind lead the blind and both fall into the ditch.' Given their economic and social position there was little peasants could do about it. Laymen above them in the social scale, whether in villages or towns, had more independence. Those fired with religious enthusiasm were bound, like pious clerics, to look outside the parish for spiritual comfort. What such men sought was the same throughout the middle ages. It was a life lived in conformity with the life of Christ; a life with few or no material possessions; a life in which man could show love for his neighbour by giving him spiritual help and consolation; a life, also, in which he could display his love and praise of God. The great strength of the church before the later middle ages, lay in its generation of movements which enabled men to lead lives of this kind. The first of these movements within our period was that of the Cistercian monks.[9]

The Cistercians originated in a reaction to the lack of spirituality of the established Benedictine monasteries, caught up as they were in the administration of their great landed possessions. The chaplain and biographer of the abbot of one of these great monasteries, Bury St Edmunds, declared with enthusiasm, 'such were the deeds of abbot Sampson, deeds worthy of immortal record and renown'. But the deeds of which he spoke consisted largely of how the abbot freed the convent from debt by shrewd business management. And when the biographer gave a New Year's gift to the abbot, it was not a devotional tract, but a list of the churches belonging to Bury St Edmunds and their annual value.[10] The first Cistercian monastery was established at Citeaux in Burgundy in 1098, by monks breaking away from a Benedictine house at Molesme, which was being caught up in much the same materialism as we see at Bury. The aim of the new order was to escape from such pressures by founding houses in remote areas. There it would be easier to live lives of Christ-like poverty and simplicity.

In England, the two most famous houses, Rievaulx and Fountains, were established in 1131 and 1132 in remote, wild, uncultivated Yorkshire valleys. The monks, helped by lay brothers, had to clear and till the land themselves. The buildings they erected, including their conventual churches, were free of all comforts and decoration. Life there was austere, but it also provided splendid opportunities to display both love of God and man. Ailred, Rievaulx's greatest abbot, declared:

> It is the singular and unique glory of the house of Rievaulx that above all else it teaches tolerance of the weak and compassion with others in their difficulties. All whether weak or strong shall find in Rievaulx a haunt of peace and a home of perfect love of God and neighbour.

Ailred's pattern, in all his activity, was the imitation of Christ, and the phrase 'for Christ's love' came to his lips, again and again, on his death bed.[11]

Given this spiritual atmosphere, and the dearth of it elsewhere in the English church, it is not surprising that the spread of the Cistercians was phenomenal. By 1153 there were thirty-six houses. At Rievaulx itself, largely under Abbot Ailred, the number of monks and lay brothers rose from 25 in 1132 to 650 in 1165. Such rapid growth was in some ways a mixed blessing. The large number of recruits made it very difficult for the monasteries to maintain the rigid

9.3. Rievaulx Abbey

discipline and high enthusiasm of the first founders. By the early thirteenth century, the houses were already settling down to a respectable mediocrity, supported by the lucrative sheep farming on the new land which they had cleared. From the point of view of the general health of the church, however, this decline was the less serious because it was balanced, in the 1200s, by the foundation of a new movement which, in some ways, took the place of the Cistercians.

The friars began as a reaction to the worldliness and materialism of the contemporary church. In common with the Cistercians, they aspired to live in imitation of Christ; but they differed from the Cistercians in attempting to do this in the world itself, rather than by withdrawing from it.[12] St Dominic had originally conceived of his followers as a highly trained preaching order to combat heresy in France. The Franciscans aimed above all to teach by their example of Christ-like poverty. Their rule laid down that:

> the brothers shall possess nothing, neither a house, nor a place, nor anything, but as pilgrims and strangers in this world, serving God in poverty and humility, they shall seek alms, and not be ashamed, for the Lord made himself poor in this world for us.[13]

9.4. St Francis of Assisi

Both orders had a remarkable success in attracting recruits. Within fifty years of their arrival in England in the 1220s, forty-seven Dominican houses had been established and forty-nine Franciscan, usually in large towns. Each of these houses, which the orders did not own, contained about forty friars, who went out each day to preach, teach and beg.

In the church between the twelfth and thirteenth centuries, therefore, despite the depressing parochial situation, there was much vigorous spirituality to be found with the Cistercians, and latterly the friars. Indeed, the preaching of the friars went at least some way to compensate for the failure of the parish priests. Why then, did the church of the later middle ages cease to contain such elements of spirituality; and how, consequently, was the way prepared for the ideas of Wycliffe and the Lollards, ideas which the church condemned as heretical?

The decline of the friars, like that of the Cistercians, was rapid. Their houses became comfortable establishments; their begging a business somewhat akin to a modern fund-raising enterprise. The picture of the friar in the Prologue to Chaucer's *Canterbury Tales* is highly unflattering. He preferred to associate with the wealthy, and with tavern keepers and sellers of food, rather than with lepers and paupers. He was more concerned with extracting money than with true penitence. 'Therefore', Chaucer concluded, 'instead of weeping and of prayers, men must give silver to the poor friars.' Signs of disillusion can be seen as early as the 1240s, when a leading English friar, William of Nottingham, prayed that 'the gentle Jesus would raise up a new order to give new Life to our order'.[14]

It was, however, precisely a major new order to replace the friars that the later medieval church could neither conceive nor allow. We can see much of the reason for this if we go back and consider the church's reaction to the first friars in the 1200s. It was, in many quarters, a reaction of great hostility. The friars were resented because they criticised the church's wealth: because, in founding houses in towns, they threatened the positions there of established Benedictine monasteries; because, in travelling the country preaching, hearing confessions and taking burials, they encroached on the prerogatives of parish priests. While some bishops welcomed the friars as preachers, others disliked their apparent immunity from episcopal control. Although, therefore, Pope Innocent III sanctioned both the Dominicans and Franciscans, he laid down in 1215 that there should be no more new religious orders. The fact was that growth had turned the church into a great bureaucratic institution. The burden of ruling ecclesiastical affairs throughout Europe meant that the pope had become surrounded with administrative departments. Bishops, in their turn,

9.5. The confirmation of
the Order of St Francis

had a whole hierarchy of officials to help them govern their dioceses. Each of the components within the church, the pope, the bishops, the parish priests, the monasteries, and latterly the friars, were concerned, often from what seemed the best of motives, to defend their own rights and privileges. A new order, with its inevitable challenge to so many vested interests, could not be tolerated.

To understand why this situation led to the development of heresy, we need to appreciate one central point, that in their emphasis upon the need to follow Christ's example, in all its original purity, the Cistercians and the friars had much in common with heretical movements.[15] What made the church declare the latter heretical was that they went further than the friars and denied its authority, and held irregular views in matters of doctrine. The Cistercians and the friars, however, offering, as they did, some of the central ingredients of the heretical movements, yet remained perfectly orthodox and were able to deflect people from the heretical path. We can see something of

these shared ingredients if we compare the friars with the twelfth century French heretics, the Waldensians, founded by Peter Waldo.[16] Like the friars, their aim was to live in imitation of Christ. Like them they emphasised poverty and preaching, and like them they were based in the towns. The Waldensians were sometimes called the 'preaching brothers', or 'the poor men of Lyons', the town from which Peter Waldo came. What ensured that the church would condemn the Waldensians as heretical was that they also rejected the authority of the Catholic priesthood, which, of course, the friars did not. So long as the church contained within it movements which witnessed to the essentials of a life lived in conformity with Christ's, many felt there was little point in taking the dangerous extra step of rejecting the church's authority.

The first friars therefore restrained the development of heresy, canalising the energies and aspirations of those who might otherwise have embraced it. By the 1370s, in contrast, when John Wycliffe was developing his ideas, conditions were very different.[17] The church branded Wycliffe as heretical because he denied the authority of the pope and priesthood, and rejected transubstantiation. Apart from this, his ideas had much in common with those of the friars. He condemned the wealth and materialism of the church, and stressed the need to return to the purity of Christ's example: a Christ, as he wrote, who was 'busy to preach the Gospel', and 'was a poor man from his birth to his death and shunned worldly riches'.[18] Had the friars retained their early enthusiasm, they would have diverted many from the Wycliffite heresy. As it was, the reverse happened. Friars, disillusioned with their order, left it to become followers of Wycliffe. As one of them explained,

> I was a Friar full many a day
> But when I saw that their living
> Accorded not to their preaching,
> Off I cast my friar's clothing.[19]

Wycliffe's views found widespread support in the University of Oxford, where he taught, in towns like Leicester and Bristol, and among influential sections of the gentry.[20] Significantly, the church's only reaction was persecution and repression. For the moment this was successful, partly because the Lollards, as Wycliffe's followers were called, became tainted with the suspicion of political sedition.[21] In the long run, however, persecution was no answer. The continuing lack of spirituality in the church ensured that the ideas of reformation would receive a warm welcome in England.

9.6. Pope Boniface VIII and his cardinals

Further Reading

D. Knowles, *The Religious Orders in England*, vol. I (Cambridge, 1948); *The Monastic Order in England* (2nd edn, Cambridge, 1963); and *Thomas Becket* (London, 1970); C.H. Lawrence (ed.), *The English Church and the Papacy in the Middle Ages* (London, 1965); J.R.H. Moorman, *Church Life in England in the Thirteenth Century* (Cambridge, 1945).

CHAPTER TEN

The King's Peace

John Post

The popular images of medieval lawlessness are very familiar. One of them, Robin Hood, was himself a medieval creation, a romantic myth of the fugitive hero who used the wild greenwoods as a base for guerrilla warfare.[1] Sometimes the oppressors are robber barons, riding out from grim castles to pillage the unlucky peasants of the surrounding countryside. Sometimes they are more organised groupings of lords and gentry. Always it is assumed that neither social controls nor strong government prevented violence by the strong and exploitation of the weak.

This is not altogether a false picture, but it fails to include some fundamental developments in law and order which were among the most distinctive contributions made by this period to succeeding centuries. By the end of the fifteenth century, England and Wales had an elaborate and workable system of judicial bureaucracy. On the eve of the Norman Conquest, however, the enforcement of the law had looked very different.

For centuries, throughout Britain, the basis of social control had been the bloodfeud. The Celtic peoples of Scotland and Wales, and the Anglo-Saxons in England, had shared with their cousins and neighbours on mainland Europe a simple principle: that if a wrong was done, the victim or his kin had the right to claim satisfaction and compensation from the offender or his kin. This was not an excuse for opposing kin groups to carry an undying hatred from generation to generation – quite the reverse. The classic bloodfeud was a customary system which meant that even serious and violent disputes could be resolved by recognised scales of compensation. The ninth century laws of Alfred the Great, for example, and the tenth century laws of the Welsh king, Hywel the Good, gave lists of the amends to be made for injuries inflicted: Alfred's laws include ten shillings for indecent assault, and thirty shillings for loss of an ear. The community, through its elders and chieftains, compelled payment of the compensation to the victim or the victim's kin, and the matter was then publicly regarded as closed. Any further revenge counted as a fresh wrong.

At the time of the Norman Conquest these customary controls of the feud were essential ingredients of traditional laws throughout Britain. Yet the development of the law in the next few centuries was very different in England from what it was in Wales or Scotland.[2] In England a highly advanced territorial settlement was moving social loyalties away from kin towards neighbourhood; this meant that the regulated bloodfeud was less and less appropriate to English society, and the way was already open to the rule of law by public authority. In late Anglo-Saxon times there had been a trend towards a strong and bureaucratic style of kingship. The Norman Conquest gave this trend fresh impetus, especially in the field of law and legal administration.

10.1. Edward I: a contemporary 'portrait' from a legal record

An all important transition took place, from private compensation to a system which punished crime as an offence against public order. It took place in a period for which few records survive, but we know that William the Conqueror, and in the twelfth century Henry I and Henry II, all contributed to a centralised and standardised justice. By about 1200 'the king's peace' was a dominant factor in the law. There were still plenty of local variations in the law and its administration;[3] there were still plenty of ways in which individuals could initiate prosecutions against criminals or private enemies. But crime in the modern sense – murder, arson, robbery, and so on – had become the business of the king. The crown would prosecute, in the royal courts, when crime was suspected, and defendants would be liable on conviction to suffer death (for serious offences) or fines (for lesser offences), rather than to compensate the victim or his kin.

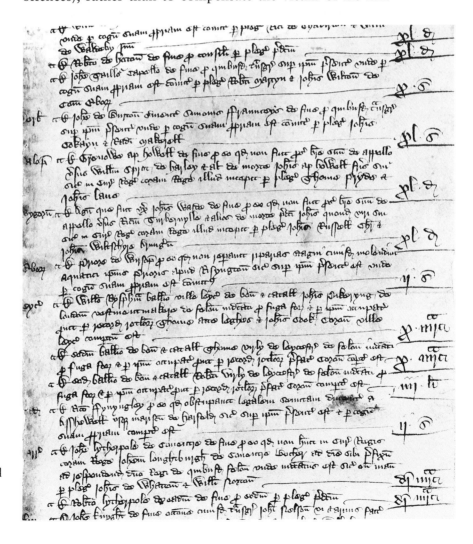

10.2. List of fines levied from offenders in the Court of the King's Bench

This transition helped, and was helped by, financial interests; money was one of the main reasons why justice was administered at all. The king, or the court-holding lord, was entitled to keep the fines paid for minor offences, and also to confiscate the possessions of anyone convicted of a capital offence. Court records always noted carefully the money due from each case, and financial officials were then instructed to collect it. There are plenty of signs that profit, rather than peace-keeping, was seen as the purpose of the exercise.

These developments of royal interest in justice meant that the administration had to become more systematic and complex. From the twelfth century onwards, royal judges went on circuit to every part of the kingdom, and soon the assize justices were regularly trying prisoners at every county goal.[4] At the same time the crown experimented with lay magistrates, to hold 'sessions of the peace' four times a year, as a royal alternative to private local courts.[5] In the fourteenth century, quarter sessions for minor offences, and assizes for serious crime, became firmly established, and remained the standard criminal courts until 1971.

These were practical arrangements, but the crown also ensured that the idea of royal justice was clothed in formality. There is a manuscript illumination of King's Bench (the highest common-law court, based at Westminster), in session around 1460.[6] (See page 171.) The scene is easily recognisable: the prisoners at the back awaiting trial, the lawyers and clerical staff accommodated comfortably in the body of the court, and the king's judges, elevated in spendour, powerful and remote.

Arrangements like these for trying criminals are familiar in many ways, but this does not mean that by 1200 the judicial machinery was modern in all essentials. Below the level of quarter sessions, there was a hierarchy of local courts, some run by the sheriff on behalf of the crown, but mostly run by or on behalf of private landowners. At the simplest level, each manor had its own court, held by the lord of the manor or his steward; this dealt with minor offences such as straying cattle, or selling bad beer. At a higher level, each county was divided into hundreds, some consisting of a single manor, others consisting of many. A court was held regularly in each hundred and, twice a year, there was an opportunity to make accusations about any serious crimes committed in the area. A record of these indictments, together with the suspects if they had been caught, was sent to the county gaol to be tried when the king's justices next visited. Because these courts were run in different ways by different authorities their effectiveness was very variable. Each court had officials who were supposed to carry out its business, but in the typical village this might mean a small handful of part-time constables, with perhaps a lock-up for emergency use. There was no organised police force.

Although the administration of justice was so uneven and diversified, all the courts had one thing in common – an increasing need for paperwork. One of the reasons why the period around 1200 is so important is that legal record-keeping began to be taken seriously; instead of having to rely on law codes and anecdotes in chronicles, the historian can at last see the law operating in individual cases.[7] By 1400 or 1450, the bureaucracy of justice was leaving a vast detritus of written records; royal and private courts were filing thousands of writs and indictments, and enrolling cases on hundreds of parchment membranes, every year.

The record of a case is almost always terse and formal. For example:

Wakelin the son of Ranulf killed Matilda Day with a knife. The village, and twelve jurors, testify that he was caught in the act with

10.3. Legal records

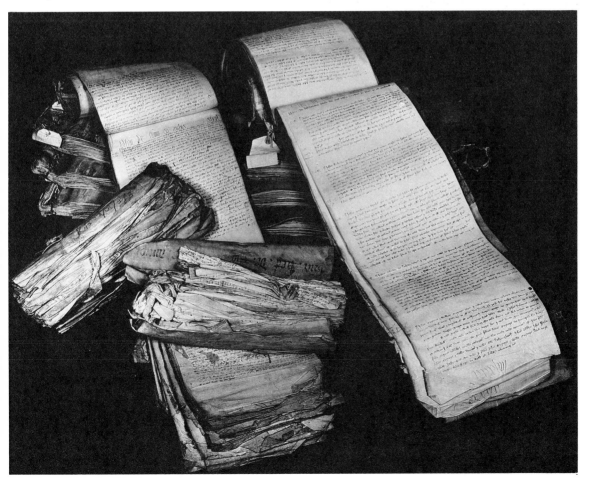

10.4. Record of the trial of Wakelin the son of Ranulf

a bloodstained knife, and so it cannot be denied. He is to be hanged. He had no possessions.

Countless thousands of entries like this, some with more detail, some with less, offer quite a detailed picture of the rule of law in a supposedly lawless society.

The picture is perhaps surprising, for the system, however ramshackle, did what in principle it was designed to do; year in, year out, the machinery of justice identified, caught, tried, and punished ordinary criminals. Every county gaol had its stock of prisoners on remand, arrested on suspicion or perhaps caught redhanded by members of the public. Energetic officials and watchful neighbours evidently went some way towards policing the community.

Arresting a criminal in the act was the most obvious way of catching him. It was the duty of every citizen to shout the alarm – raise the hue and cry – at any breach of the peace, and it was the duty of anyone hearing the hue to join in and try to catch the offender. Sometimes this process amounted to nothing more than neighbours taking official notice of a drunken brawl, but on other occasions whole groups of passers-by chased and caught dangerous criminals.

Even if the hue and cry was not successful, or was not raised because the crime was committed by stealth, criminals were often tracked down by other means. There was certainly no forensic detection, but the authorities were able to use witnesses and informers to help identify suspects, and then to use the slow but elaborate bureaucracy to organise arrests. In 1248, for example, two foreign merchants were robbed of a large sum of money at Alton in Hampshire, a notoriously dangerous spot for travellers. They petitioned the king for help, and the subsequent investigations were enormously successful; despite some well-connected skulduggery and a local conspiracy of silence, at least twenty-five people were convicted of involvement in the robbery, and several were hanged.[8] In 1390 Geoffrey Chaucer, travelling in his capacity as a civil servant, was mugged at New Cross; inquiries identified the culprits and they were brought to trial.[9] The vast body of surviving case records shows that far less glamorous cases were regularly pursued just as effectively.

Prosecutions relied a good deal on criminals who turned informer in the hope of a temporary reprieve. William Rose, a horse-thief who was

10.5. Confessions and accusations of William Rose

arrested in Winchester in 1389, gained seven years' reprieve before he was hanged. His original statement survives, complete with corrections and afterthoughts; despite the official jargon in which it was written down, it conveys some of the flavour of his career – moving in a criminal underworld, never very successful, and always on the run. But from the official point of view his statement was a working document; he accused more than fifty people, and at least a dozen of them were caught and convicted. Informers like this compensated in part for inefficiencies elsewhere in the system.

A more orderly procedure involved communal accusation. In the absence of a police force or a public prosecutor, courts began in the twelfth century to use the jury of presentment – that is, jurors sworn to accuse anyone suspected of crime in their area.[10] This came to be the main source of indictments which actually came to trial, and by about 1400 it had almost completely superseded earlier procedures based on private accusation.

The criminal trial itself saw some important changes. Traditional modes of proof had put less emphasis on the ascertainable facts of the case, and more on the defendant's reputation with God and his neighbours. God's judgement was invoked in two ways: by ordeal, and by battle. In the ordeal, the defendant was made to undergo a severe physical test.[11] For example, he might be made to pick up a hot iron weight; if, after three days in bandages, the burns on his hand had healed, it was taken as a sign that he was innocent. In trial by battle, the defendant faced his accuser in single combat, usually with blunted weapons; if he was beaten, he was taken to be guilty. There is a sketch of one such duel, between an informer and one of his victims, fighting to see which of them would end on the gallows in the background. The underlying principle in each type of proof was that God would preserve the innocent unharmed, but not the guilty. Eventually the church objected, and trial by ordeal was abolished in 1215. Trial by battle declined rapidly, although it was not abolished until 1819.

What took over from these archaic proofs was trial by jury. The older procedures had included oath-helpers, who were essentially friends and neighbours called by the defendant to swear that he was a true and honest person. By the early thirteenth century, however, the group of jurors was (in theory) neutral, chosen by the court, and their job was to swear to the defendant's guilt or innocence of the specified crime. At first they were expected to decide on their own local knowledge of reputations and events, but gradually they came to decide on the basis of evidence presented to them, and it was this sort of trial by jury that was enshrined as a civil right in Magna Carta. These changes did not guarantee a fair trial; the laws of evidence were

10.6. Trial by battle
from a legal record

crude, and the courts often gave defendants very little benefit of such rights as they had.[12] Nevertheless, the general shape of the English criminal trial was slowly emerging.

For the defendant who was convicted, the possible fates were very limited; after the Norman Conquest, sentencing was simplified and often harsh.[13] Serious crimes were categorised as felonies, and the only punishment available was death. For minor offences it was normal to pay a fine. Since the theft of goods worth more than a shilling was a felony, many people could be, and were, hanged for stealing quite small items. There was no convict imprisonment to allow for variable sentencing; it was difficult enough to organise effective custody for prisoners awaiting trial, without the increased problems and expenses that prison sentences would have caused.

One way of avoiding these harsh procedures was to evade arrest. If an accused person failed to answer repeated summonses, he could then be declared an outlaw – a person with no legal status or rights. This did not necessarily make him a fugitive. Many people were able to ignore the fact that they had been outlawed (even supposing that they heard about it), but in theory they could have been beheaded on sight, and this sometimes happened to notorious criminals. If the prototype Robin Hood ever existed, he may well have had something to fear.

On the other hand, there were some legitimate escape routes for the guilty. Courts could be very sympathetic towards a defendant. It was quite common for the jury to say that stolen goods were worth less than a shilling, thus averting the death penalty. In cases of homicide, it is surprising how often the jury blamed the dead person for starting the fight. Sometimes it is possible to detect a hanging judge or a corrupted jury, but in general the balance of convictions and acquittals suggests that verdicts may have been based genuinely on the facts of the cases and the merits of the defendants.

It was also possible to plead 'benefit of clergy'. This was based on the fact that clergymen could not be executed; instead, they were handed over to the ecclesiastical authorities. For this purpose, the definition of a clergyman was decided by a very simple literacy test, and it was not too difficult for an intelligent defendant to claim his benefit of clergy and take his chance in the bishop's prison.

Another option was the charter of pardon. Originally, kings granted pardons in exceptional cases, such as homicides by lunatics. But it soon became obvious that there were advantages in granting pardons wholesale. Edward I found that pardons conditional on military service were a good way of raising an army. More often it was simply a moneymaking exercise. On the Patent Rolls there are standard forms

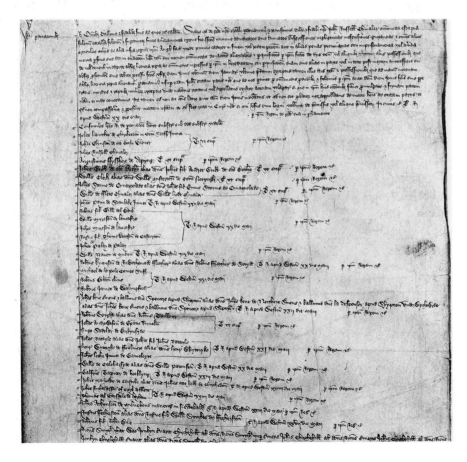

10.7. Charter of pardon and list of subscribers

of pardons, followed by great lists of people who had paid to be included. Each subscriber received his own charter of pardon, which, if produced in court, prevented any further proceedings against him. Criminals with cash in hand always had a fair chance of buying royal favour in this way.

Even allowing for these variations and exceptions, the administration of justice was far from straightforward. Powerful and influential people used both crime and the criminal law to promote their private interests. Some of the best-known examples come from the adventures of the Pastons of Norfolk. John Paston was in dispute with Lord Molyns about the ownership of the manor of Gresham. Each side in turn took over the manor by force, and seemed to think little of violence as a part of daily life; in 1448, John's wife Margaret wrote him a letter from home, with local news and a shopping list, and she said, 'I pray you to get some crossbows, for your houses here are so low that no man may shoot out there with any longbow'. Within a couple of years Molyns had sent an armed gang who threw the Pastons out; then he began to harass their friends by having false charges brought against them in the local courts.[14] Use of the legal system did not by any means imply respect for it.

What is interesting about this sort of purposeful lawlessness is that those involved did not necessarily invoke the criminal law every time they had reason to do so. At the end of the fourteenth century Sir William Bagot was a notorious local bully in his native Midlands. One of his long-term enemies, a lawyer called John Catesby, kept notes of what Bagot was doing.[15] So we know that Bagot smashed a watermill belonging to Catesby, and that in 1397 he sent a party of archers to take over one of Catesby's manors. But we also know that Catesby made no attempt to bring criminal proceedings in consequence, preferring to use private lawsuits and local politics to make his point. Both men knew that violence and the law were just two of the tactics with which personal advantage could be pursued. To the disinterested observer, however, this is just the sort of behaviour that has given the middle ages a bad name.

The governing classes were not only adept at ignoring or abusing the law; they were also well able to shape it to their own purposes, even if this was at the expense of public order. For example, it is clear that by the thirteenth century punishment for rape was not an aspect of law enforcement. In theory, rape was a felony and should have been punished accordingly. There were certainly plenty of prosecutions, but there are no recorded instances of rapists suffering the consequences. This seems to have been because many of the accusations were attempts to extract marriage, or at least compensation, from prosperous men who had ruined the prospects of poorer women in a marriage market where female virginity was a prime asset. The male-dominated courts took a dismissive view even when a forcible rape had obviously taken place, and fresh legislation in 1275 and 1285 merely resulted in fewer cases being brought.[16]

But the abuse of rape law went further than this, and became much more deliberate. Many of the so-called rapes were really elopements, and the prosecutions were initiated by members of the family who disapproved of a girl's choice of partner. This is especially clear from the story behind a further statute in 1382.[17] Sir Thomas West had spent a lifetime building up wealth and aristocratic connections, and he must have expected his daughter Eleanor to marry well. Unfortunately for him, she eloped with a soldier, Nicholas Clifton, who was not only an impoverished younger son, but a bit of a scapegrace as well. Sir Thomas was furious. He realised that the couple intended to get married, and he petitioned successfully for a new statute, which allowed next of kin to bring private prosecutions for rape, even when the woman was known to have consented to the relationship. He failed in his ambition to get his son-in-law hanged and his daughter disinherited, for Clifton bought a pardon, and Eleanor was mentioned in her mother's will. But the fact remains that rape law had been completely transformed, from the punishment of rape to the upholding of family policies. Women's sexuality, consenting or other-wise, lost all effective protection by the law.

All this evidence for the governing classes manipulating the law, or ignoring it, might suggest that in practice there was one law for the rich and one law for the poor. This is not entirely true; as we have seen,

10.8. Bequest to the Cliftons in the will of the wife of Sir Thomas West

10.9. Illustration of a fifteenth century court of law

acquittal rates in routine trials do suggest that the ordinary defendant had some chance of survival. At the other end of the scale, there are many examples of criminal gentry who failed to get away with it. In 1248, Sir John le Breton (another father who disapproved of his daughter's choice) castrated her boyfriend, and, despite his status, he was forced to go into exile. In 1388, Elizabeth Walton, who was an heiress in her own right, got her household servants to murder her husband; she used her money to get her case transferred to a higher court, but she was still burned at the stake. There were also many judges and civil servants, over the years, who were punished for corruption. But such cases stand out as exceptions, and it is likely that here the criminals had become so socially unacceptable that neither class solidarity nor an indulgent king would help them. Normally, the advantages of superior wealth and status weighed in favour of those defendants who enjoyed them.

So far, what we have seen of crime and the law has been practical in purpose – the pursuit of advantage and, as a secondary consideration, the defence of public order. But this is not quite the whole story. From the late fourteenth century onwards, there are signs that an increase in lay piety was changing the morality of the law. Witchcraft is a case in point. The idea that witches were persecuted in medieval England is nonsense; there were virtually no witchcraft trials before Tudor times. But occasionally a suggestion creeps into the records that superstitious practices were believed to enhance or promote crime (especially treason), and this alerts us to changing establishment attitudes.

More interestingly, we find that over the same period the laity was taking over the church's role as the repressor of sexual licence. Local courts began to prosecute fornication and adultery, and local authorities began to harass prostitutes, whose activities had previously been tolerated.[18] In London, people found guilty of these offences were carted in procession through the streets. The sexual activities of the supposedly celibate clergy were also tolerated less; priests were the commonest targets for the new wave of prosecutions, and in the fifteenth century there was a dramatic increase in the numbers of rape charges brought against clergymen. Most emphatically of all, there were many instances of parishioners castrating their priests. In this area the familiar patterns of legal and illegal action were apparently being used to promote spiritual rather than material ends.

Medieval society was perhaps unimaginably complex in its approach to law and order. At times, lawlessness could go unpunished and almost uncriticised; and yet people were highly conscious of the rule of law and put a good deal of effort into making it work. From this paradoxical coexistence of attitudes the middle ages saw, perhaps surprisingly, the emergence in England of a machinery of justice which remained unchanged in its essentials, and recognisable in many of its details, for six hundred years.

Further Reading

J.H. Baker, *An Introduction to English Legal History*, 2nd edn (London, 1978); J.G. Bellamy, *Crime and Public Order in England in the Later Middle Ages* (London, 1973); F. Pollock and F.W. Maitland, *The History of English Law before the time of Edward I*, 2nd edn, reissue (Cambridge, 1968); R.B. Pugh, *Imprisonment in Medieval England* (Cambridge, 1968).

The Written Word:

from Domesday Book to Caxton

M.T. Clanchy

It was in the middle ages that the foundations of modern literacy were laid. Medieval people were fascinated by the power of writing and harnessed it to a variety of purposes. In remote island monasteries, like Lindisfarne and Iona, Celtic and Anglo-Saxon monks had pioneered the writing of illuminated texts of the scripture. The Anglo-Saxons had also used writing for more ordinary purposes like recording the boundaries of property in charters. After the Norman Conquest these traditions continued and extended: skills in literacy spread from monks and royal clerks to knights and their ladies, merchants and artisans, and even to some peasants. By the time Caxton introduced printing to England in the 1470s, perhaps as much as half the population could read. How had this been achieved, and what did it signify?

The way we speak is different from the way we write and this was as true in the middle ages as it is today. At school it is impressed on us that we must write things down 'properly', that is, words must be correctly spelt and sentences must be grammatical. We do not talk as 'properly' as that, of course, and neither did the Anglo-Saxons. They spoke a variety of dialects, which were scarcely comprehensible from one part of the country to another. When they came to write, on the other hand, they, like us, were taught to write 'properly': either in a specially standardised form of Old English or in Latin. The Norman conquerors in 1066 likewise spoke a variety of languages and dialects: they were not all French speakers, as there were Bretons and Flemings among them. But their leaders shared a uniform written language, as all their writing was done in Latin.

Essentially Latin was *the* language of literacy. To be 'literate' (*literatus*) meant to know Latin because the holy scripture, and anything else of importance, was written down in that language. The Norman conquerors therefore ignored the Anglo-Saxons' peculiar habit of doing some of their writing in Old English. Norman clerics, headed by Archbishop Lanfranc who had been educated in Italy, made their records in Latin, as that was the most 'proper' way to write and it brought England into line with western Christendom.

William the Conqueror's Domesday Book set the seal on the conquest. It demonstrated the power of writing in Latin and the power of the Normans. Everything of value was listed. Its scope is shown in this single line describing part of the village of Wanborough in Surrey:

Ibi ecclesia (there is a church) & *viii servi* (and 8 serfs) & *vi acrae prati* (and 6 acres of meadow). *Silva* (a wood) *de xxx porcis* (for 30 pigs).[1]

We can almost see the little church, in its meadow with the wood beyond, and the serfs who now worked for a Norman master. 'So very narrowly did the king make this investigation that not one ox nor one cow nor one pig was left out.'[2] That statement is a pardonable exaggeration in the Anglo-Saxon Chronicle.

The pages of Domesday Book are beautifully laid out in the abbreviated script which was the standard way of writing Latin. The generous margins, headings in capitals, and underlining in red (rubrics), made it easy to look things up. The book was called 'Domesday' because it terrified the 'natives', who were reminded of the Last Judgement, when the book of Revelation would be opened to show the names of the saved and the damned. In many medieval

11.1. Detail from Domesday Book

11.2. Part of the initial from the beginning of the Book of Genesis, the Winchester Bible

churches and manuscripts, Christ was depicted seated in majesty above the firmament holding the book of Judgement. In the same way William the Conqueror sat beyond time and space on his throne, with Domesday Book as his symbol of power and achievement.

In comparing Domesday Book with the bible, contemporaries were thinking of the great illuminated manuscripts kept in major churches. The tradition of monks making precious books flourished after the Norman Conquest as much as before. The Winchester Bible was made for Henry of Blois, the princely bishop who was King Stephen's brother. A single capital 'I', the initial of *Incipit* meaning 'Here begins', contains the whole history of mankind, from Adam and Eve and Noah's Ark down to the birth of Christ and the Last Judgement at the world's end. The act of writing was a sacred labour, likened by monks to ploughing the fields: 'the pages are ploughed by the divine letters and the seed of God's word is planted in the parchment which ripens into crops of completed books (*libri perfecti* – 'perfect books')'.[3] These are the words of Peter the Venerable, abbot of Cluny, the great monastery in Burgundy, where Henry of Blois had been trained.

The writers of such books knew that they were doing something important and they were not modest about their achievements, despite being monks. Eadwin of Canterbury is depicted in the conventional pose of a scribe, with a pen in his right hand and penknife in the left. The strange blues and greens in this portrait are not intended to be realistic. Around the frame is an inscription beginning:

Scriptorum princeps ego – I am the prince of writers, neither my praise nor my fame will die[4]

Eadwin's portrait accompanies a text of the psalms of extraordinary elaboration. This is a work of instruction as much as of worship, as it displays on the one page three variant Latin texts, together with a commentary in the margins and between the lines, and an English and a French translation. French was only just beginning to be written down in the twelfth century and this is one of the earliest recorded pieces of French prose. Paradoxically, the conquered English were pioneers in the writing of French.

Eadwin's work also illustrates the medieval practice of writing explanatory commentaries, or 'glosses' as they were called, around a text. The words of the psalm itself are almost overwhelmed by the accumulation of learning on all sides. Although the glosses look incomprehensible, they were an efficient research tool, presenting the scholar with text and commentary simultaneously for comparison. At the time Eadwin was writing (in the middle of the twelfth century) the

11.3. Eadwin, 'prince of writers'

11.4. Three parallel texts, with glosses and translations, from Eadwin's text of the psalms

11.5. Griffith falling to his death from the Tower of London, drawn by Matthew Paris

schoolmen, in theology at Paris and law at Bologna, were producing new glosses from their own lectures. Ultimately the initiative in writing and learning moved from monasteries to the universities: in England's case to Oxford and Cambridge and in Scotland to St Andrews. But this was a slow process and the writing procedures developed by monks like Eadwin continued until after the invention of printing.

The greatest writer in Britain in the monastic tradition, in every sense a writer, was Matthew Paris of St Albans who died in 1259. He is best known as an historian of England in Henry III's reign, but his works surpass conventional chronicle writing in their mass of detail and range of interest. He was as concerned with world events, like the coming of the Mongols, as he was with the privileges and history of St Albans. He drew maps and an itinerary showing each stage of a journey from London to Sicily. This was compiled when Henry III was hoping to make his son king of Sicily. Like a true monk, Matthew wrote out his works in his own hand and embellished them in a variety of ways. His sketches of towns on the road from London to Calais (the first stage of the journey to Sicily) are conventional diagrams, while in his chronicle he took the unusual step of illustrating events. In one dramatic little drawing, Griffith, a son of Llywelyn the Great, prince of Wales, escapes from the Tower of London and falls headlong in the attempt. The knotted sheets, on which he depended, dangle from the battlements.

Matthew Paris's drawings were functional, as well as being entertaining. They were signposts which helped the reader to find his place. Like all illustrations in books, they also helped to bridge the gap between readers and non-readers by showing what the text was about and making it look attractive. Monks had centuries of experience of displaying their work to the kings and other great laymen upon whose goodwill and gifts they depended. Monks were the mediators of literacy to the laity. They introduced the laity to the idea that their gifts should be recorded in writing, so that they would be remembered for ever like the scripture itself. So the benefactors of Crowland abbey, with the king at their head, crowd forward to place their charters on the altar of their patron saint. Each charter specifies a different gift of land.

A rich collection of documents of this sort is preserved in the Prior's Kitchen at Durham cathedral, which was dedicated to St Cuthbert. One charter has a broken knife handle attached to it and the text explains that this is the knife of Stephen of Bulmer's steward offered to St Cuthbert as a *signum* or 'sign' of his gift to the monks. Stephen was a local knight who was presumably illiterate. Just as Matthew Paris signposted his text for his readers and non-readers, so the

11.6. The benefactors of Crowland Abbey, crowding forward with their charters

Durham monks accepted Stephen's 'sign' of a knife and they attached an explanatory text to it. A commoner way for a person to 'sign' a document was with a seal bearing his name or with an autograph cross. In one charter from Durham, Adam Fitz Ilbert is represented as a knight on his seal and he has also made the sign of the cross on the document itself: 'I Adam have subscribed this sign of the holy cross with my own hand'.[5] The cross does not necessarily mean that Adam was unable to write. It was a 'sign' of sacredness, not of illiteracy. The seal similarly functioned like a cashline or autoteller card at a bank; it enabled its user to draw on his resources without signing his name. Both cross and seal, like all signs, also had the effect of uniting literate and illiterate, as they enabled their users to participate in the writing process without actually forming letters themselves.

Seals and autograph crosses look like a good way both of authenticating documents and of getting lay people involved in writing. But the process was not so straightforward, as many charters were forged by the monks themselves because writing was so

11.7. Forged charter in the name of the first Norman bishop of Durham

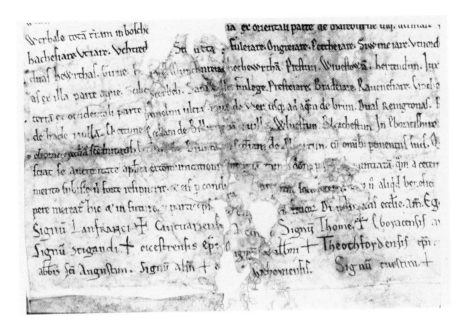

important to them. One, issued in the name of the first Norman bishop of Durham, looks like the real thing. Distinguished prelates subscribe their crosses: Lanfranc of Canterbury, Thomas of York, and many others. But the charter is dated AD 1093, when most of these signatories were dead. What did the monks of Durham think they were doing? The answer is: nothing very different from what they usually did. The charter is described as being made in the presence of St Cuthbert himself. He was a living presence for the monks and they had to ensure that their saint kept hold of his property. They wrote out this title-deed for him in much the same way as they wrote up miracles at his shrine to prove and reinforce his power. Penning – or forging, as we would say – a charter for St Cuthbert was as much a sacred labour as embellishing the letters of scripture themselves.

The distinction between a charter and a sacred book, between the documentary proof of a past gift and future hope illuminated in scripture, could be a fine one. Charters were sometimes written into books, so that they too were enfolded in scripture. Occasionally they were illuminated, like the Kelso abbey charter. Within the initial 'M', Malcolm, king of Scots sits enthroned alongside his predecessor, David I. Whereas David has a venerable beard and sits bolt upright, Malcolm is depicted as a beardless youth, in a relaxed attitude resting the sword of state on his lap. The serpents represent the power of evil. This image has as full and important a message as the text of the charter. It recalls the serpent in the Garden of Eden and the institution of kings in the Old Testament to rule fallen man with the sword of justice. This is a 'sign' or *signum* for the kings of Scots, making them equal in dignity with the kings of England or France. (See page 73.)

There was no sharp distinction between saintly or kingly mystique on the one hand and the business routines on the other, which monks and royal clerks created in the twelfth century in order to harness writing to their financial needs. Money is as indispensable as virtue, explained Richard Fitz Nigel in the treatise in which he expounded the 'sacred mysteries' (as he called them) of the exchequer.[6] The exchequer's business was tax-collecting and its earliest account, or 'pipe roll', survives from 1130. (The pipe roll was so called because it looked like a drain-pipe when rolled up.) The pipe rolls were written in abbreviated Latin, like the other early records, and the commonest terms used are what we might expect: *deb'* (owes), *redd' compot'* (renders account), and *in thesauro* recording money paid 'into the treasury'. The sheriff of each county came annually to the exchequer to account for the money he had collected or paid out on the king's behalf; the pipe rolls record this process. They mark the beginning of bureaucracy, as they formed a continuous series building up from year to year. They still exist, in the Public Record Office in Chancery Lane, in unbroken sequence from 1156 until the nineteenth century. The most evocative of the exchequer's records are the tally sticks which served as receipts. Sums of money were represented on them by notches of different depths and shapes. For example, a deep triangular notch means £20. Through tallies, exchequer clerks made contact with the semi-literate officials in the shires, rather in the way that the monks of Durham kept Stephen of Bulmer's knife and labelled it. Tally sticks were visual and tangible 'signs' which mediated the mysteries of literacy and numeracy to the laity.

The most sophisticated keepers of written accounts were not the clerks of the English exchequer but the Italian bankers who provided credit for a variety of clients, ranging from kings to women householders. At the centre of this web of finance and bureaucracy sat the pope because his officials extended to every part of Christendom and he had to account for his stewardship. Good causes need prescribed routines, as all collectors for charity know. The papal *curia* thus became the high court of Europe, enforcing a book-bound law. Pope Boniface VIII in 1300 sits in the traditional posture of Christ in Majesty, but he is surrounded by bureaucrats and the book on his knee is more probably the canon law than holy scripture. Church courts provided a model for all others, especially in their reliance on documents. In an illustration of the court of King's Bench in the fifteenth century the judges are at the top and the wretched chained prisoners at the bottom, while the centre is dominated by the clerks' table with its inkwells and rolls of parchment. Justice was not

11.8. The Whaddon
Folio: the Court of
King's Bench

necessarily done in the middle ages, but it was certainly seen to be written down in thousands of court rolls. 'Law', wrote Bracton in his treatise in the thirteenth century, 'may in the broadest sense be said to be everything that is read'.[7]

All this writing activity, whether for religious purposes or governmental routines (or for both at once), caused more people to read. Through bureaucracy the power of writing reached down to remote villages. 'Thou art written down in my writ', a beadle says to a peasant in an English song of the fourteenth century.[8] To know whether that was really so, the peasant needed to be able to read. Every freeman in English law had the protection of writing: 'no one need answer for his freehold without a royal writ' was the fundamental rule which caused the proliferation of hundreds of thousands of writs from the thirteenth century onwards.[9] As a consequence, lay landowners began to collect documents to pass on to their children. In a book made in the 1240s, Richard Hotot of Northamptonshire kept a copy of Magna Carta and used a system of footnotes to explain the details of his rent roll. Literacy and book-learning were also encouraged by making them attractive and even covetable. A roll, which must once have belonged to a minor knightly family like Richard Hotot's, looks more fun than an account roll and yet it too has an instructional purpose, as it displays England's history through the genealogy of its kings. The portraits of the kings lead to the captions. They act as signposts, like Matthew Paris's drawings or the seals affixed to charters and writs.

Literacy was being domesticated and women played a significant part in this. They found for books a place in the home, instead of in church and court where men dominated. By the fifteenth century books had become part of the luxurious furnishings of a lady's bedchamber along with cushions, lap-dogs and casement windows. In scenes of the Annunciation, the Virgin Mary was no longer shown spinning but praying from a book. The aspirations of the lord and lady to be prayerful readers like Mary is emphasised by the matching colours: the blue and red on their prie-dieux are picked up in Mary's mantle and bookrest. This masterpiece among English miniatures was painted in about 1400. The book of hours in which it appears was made for domestic and not clerical use. Although formal teaching remained a largely male and clerical preserve throughout the middle ages, it was women who were responsible for first awakening an interest in letters in the young. That is as clear in the story of King Alfred and his mother, as it is in Chaucer's Prioress's tale, where the widow sends her 'litel clergeon', her baby clergyman, to school.[10]

Chaucer's 'litel clergeon' learned to read by chanting prayers in Latin, which seems an odd way to start to a modern mind. Beginning

11.9. The Annunciation, depicting the Virgin and the donors with books

with Latin had been the practice for centuries: essentially, to be 'literate' meant to know Latin. But by Chaucer's time the dominance of Latin was at last visibly receding, as literature was being written in a variety of European languages: most notably French, Italian, Spanish and German. Dante, who wrote his *Divine Comedy* in Italian, emphasised the paradoxes in this development by publishing in Latin in 1300 a defence of this 'vulgar eloquence'. In England at much the same time Lady Denise de Montchensy commissioned an Essex knight, Walter of Bibbesworth, to write a text to help her children learn French. This was not intended as a substitute for a grounding in Latin, but as a supplement to it. One manuscript of Walter's work takes the form of a roll with a wooden winder, small enough for the owner to carry it about in his pocket and polish up his French in idle moments. The heyday of French as a written language in England was not the years immediately after the Norman Conquest – the Normans wrote in Latin, as we have seen – but two centuries later. Between 1250 and 1350 writs and legal records began to be written in French because it was replacing Latin by then as the language of business and culture. English remained a poor third until Chaucer's time.

It was more difficult to write English than Latin, as no one agreed about the rules. The Normans had killed Old English by withdrawing the royal authority which had helped to standardise it. As a consequence, writers of what is now called Middle English used a bewildering variety of spelling and grammar because there was no one to correct them. In the twelfth and thirteenth centuries these writers were isolated pioneers, like Master Nicholas of Guildford, who probably composed *The Owl and the Nightingale*, imagining himself in a 'summer dale' (line 1), in the 1200s.[11] Until the fourteenth century, English works, however accomplished they were, did not have a wide currency. Even if a consistent dialect were adhered to by the writer, the result might only be to make his work look more peculiar in other parts of the country. This was one reason why Latin remained the foundation of reading for so long. Everyone spoke English in some form or other (apart from those who had a Celtic mother tongue) but when it came to writing something down, it was safer to spell it out 'properly' in Latin.

Why written English came into its own at the end of the fourteenth century is difficult to explain. The retreat from Latin was a European phenomenon. Chaucer was very conscious of Dante and Boccaccio, who had pioneered 'vulgar eloquence' in Italy; he did the same for England. Written English was rapidly adopted at all levels of society: from Chaucer, who had been educated in the household of the duke of Clarence, down to the persecuted Lollards who pioneered English texts of the bible. The same thing happened in Scotland, where John Barbour, archdeacon of Aberdeen, wrote in praise of Robert Bruce and the king himself, James I, was an innovative poet in his own right. In England, during the Peasants' Revolt in 1381, John Ball, the dissident priest, wrote cryptic messages in English, while Thomas Walsingham, the St Albans chronicler, departed from his Latin text to record:

John Shep[herd], sometime priest of St Mary's York, and now of Colchester, greeteth well John Nameless and John the Miller and

11.10. The Gutenberg Bible

11.11. The Psalter of 1457: the earliest dated printed book

John Carter . . . Stand together in God's name and biddeth Piers Ploughman go to his work.[12]

Ball's reference to Piers Ploughman connects popular rebellion with the new literature in English, as Langland's massive poem of that name describes the visions and searchings of the truthful labouring man.

English displaced Latin in the fifteenth century even in such a conservative type of document as a monastic cartulary. One from a convent explains that:

Women of religion, in reading books, of Latin, be excused of great understanding, as it is not their mother tongue.[13]

So the charters were translated into English. Paradoxically the decline of literacy, in the medieval sense of knowing Latin, was accompanied by an advance in literacy, in the modern sense of reading and writing one's mother tongue. Perhaps as much as half the population could read a little English or Scots by 1500, although the number who could write must have been much smaller.

This growth in literacy is often thought to have begun with the invention of printing, but that puts things the wrong way round. Printing would not have been successful unless there was a market for it. In other words, there had to be a lot of people who were already reading and demanding books. Seen in the perspective of medieval writing, the invention of printing in the fifteenth century was the end-point or culmination of a thousand years of book-production and growth in the techniques of literacy. The middle ages had produced the most magnificent books ever made and Gutenberg, the German inventor of printing, had difficulty matching their quality. He almost succeeded in the so-called 'Gutenberg Bible'. It looks just like a medieval manuscript, as does the earliest dated printed book, the psalter produced by Gutenberg's former partner in 1457. It was no coincidence that the books of the Latin bible were the first printed works. The inventors of printing went for the most prestigious and traditional product, the illumination of scripture. They automated the scribe and made the treasures of a millennium of religious culture available to domestic buyers. This was the first market for printing. The earliest job-printing likewise cashed in on tradition in the shape of the mass production of indulgence forms. Like charters for monasteries, these promised their purchasers profit in the next world (in the form of absolution from sin) in exchange for a cash gift.

11.12. Printed indulgence form of 1455

Caxton too was a business man and the earliest dated printing done on his press was likewise an indulgence form in Latin, filled in on 13 December 1476. But this was an exception. Caxton specialised in English works in order to get a corner of the market, for continental printers already had a head-start in Latin. He himself translated a huge amount from French (more than 4,500 printed pages) and he also published the great English authors, starting with Chaucer's *Canterbury Tales*.

With the invention of printing the history of writing enters a new phase. Printing marks the beginning of mass production and this destroyed the art of the medieval scribe. Many more people learned to write, but they could not write like Eadwin, the 'prince of writers'. Medieval manuscripts now sell for tens of thousands of pounds because the culture that produced them is beyond recovery. The historian's job is to recall and interpret the achievements of the past: to look back, and not forward along some imagined line of progress. In that long perspective we can see what we owe to the middle ages. The monks gave us the ideal of the book and of literacy as a high endeavour, while the clerks with their rolls and writs made writing into an instrument of government.

Further Reading

J. Backhouse, *The Illuminated Manuscript* (Oxford, 1979); N.F. Blake, *Caxton England's First Publisher* (London, 1976); M.T. Clanchy, *From Memory to Written Record: England 1066–1307* (London, 1979); J. Coleman, *English Literature in History 1350–1400* (London, 1981); L.C. Hector, *The Handwriting of English Documents* (London, 1958); S.G. Bell 'Medieval Women Book-Owners' *Signs* 7 (1982) pp. 742–68.

Europe and the Wider World

Geoffrey Parker

In the year 1589 Richard Hakluyt, the first historian of English overseas expansion, published a famous book entitled *The principall navigations, voiages and discoveries of the English nation*. He began, in suitably chauvinistic fashion, as follows:

> [Just] as in all former ages, [the English] have been men full of activity, stirrers abroad and searchers of the remote part of the world, so in this most famous and peerless government of her most excellent Majesty [Queen Elizabeth I], her subjects . . . in searching the most opposite corners and quarters of the world . . . have excelled all the nations and people of the earth.[1]

It was stirring stuff and, with England's defeat of the Spanish Armada still fresh in their minds, the Queen's subjects loved it. The book was expanded and reprinted in three volumes within ten years. Knowing, as we do today, that England's seaborne exploits eventually resulted in an empire on which the sun never set, it is tempting to see English expansion as Hakluyt did: as a smooth, continuous process – if not 'in *all* former ages', then certainly stretching back to the voyages to Newfoundland and Labrador undertaken, during the reign of Henry VII, by John Cabot and the men of Bristol.

There were, of course, some attempts to secure direct access from the British Isles to the wealth of the Orient, but their significance is usually exaggerated. John Cabot, a Genoese who was convinced that one could sail westwards direct from Europe to Asia, persuaded Henry VII of England to back a voyage from Bristol to 'the country of the Great Khan' in 1497. He discovered Labrador. Although Cabot was lost on a subsequent voyage, other Bristol merchants continued his efforts to discover a westerly way straight to the Orient. Of course,

12.1. Sebastian Cabot

they failed. Yet even when it became inescapably obvious that an entirely new continent, America, lay in between Europe and Asia, the men of Bristol still concentrated on attempts to outflank it by searching for a 'north-west passage'. Sebastian Cabot, son of John, discovered the entrance to Hudson's Bay in 1508–9; subsequent Bristol voyages in 1528 and 1536 further explored the coast of Labrador.[2]

But not one of these ventures proved to be a commercial success. The coastline of northern America simply had too little to offer the pioneers: no luxuries, no treasure, not even a passage to India. Efforts to break into the trading system established by the Iberian powers further south totally failed. Although William Hawkins, founder of a famous naval dynasty, sailed both to the Spanish Canaries and to Portuguese Brazil in search of trade, he failed to find it; the Iberians froze him out. But as long as Antwerp, the universal emporium across the North Sea, remained open to English and Scottish merchants, there was little need to look elsewhere.

The city on the Scheldt became, in the first half of the sixteenth century, one of the great centres of world trade. Its population grew

12.2. Antwerp in the early sixteenth century

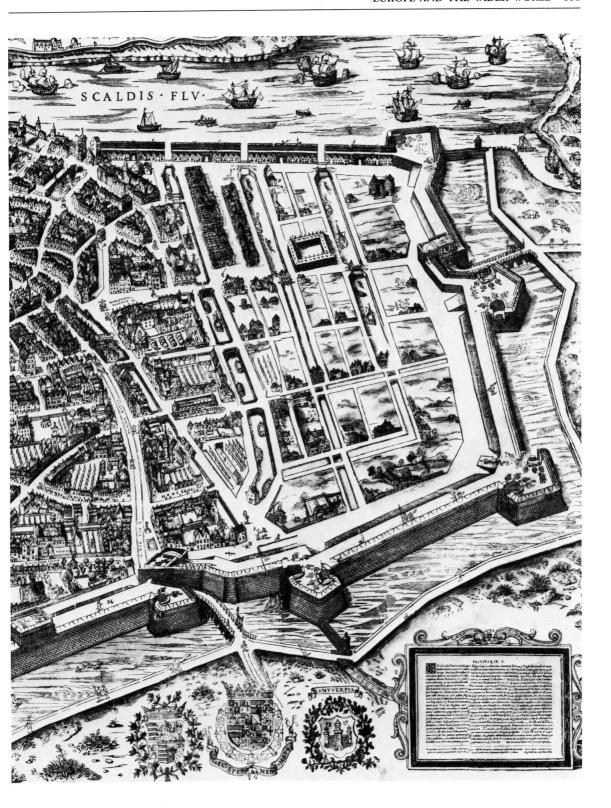

from 47,000 in 1496 to 100,000 by 1560. Its harbour was always packed with shipping; its stock exchange was ceaselessly active. Not only were Portuguese merchants to be found there: Antwerp also welcomed the English staple (with some 200 residents), the German 'Hessenhuis', and communities from many other European nations. The Scots, too, were not far away. In 1541, they opened a trade centre at Veer, one of Antwerp's outports, which long remained the staple of their overseas commerce. By 1550, some 90 per cent of our island's exports were channelled to the Scheldt, largely through the east coast ports, and above all, in the case of England, through London.[3]

It was, paradoxically, precisely this ease of access to the rich Antwerp market that seems to have limited the role played by the peoples of Britain in the great discoveries. After all, if the attractive products of Asia, Africa and America could all be bought cheaply and abundantly in the Low Countries, what was the point of risking life, limb and ship in sailing halfway round the world oneself? The principal navigations, voyages and discoveries of the English nation – and of the Scots and Irish – still lay in the future.

It was the states of the Iberian peninsula, not those of the British Isles, which led Europe's overseas expansion. The discovery of a sea route to India by the Portuguese, and to America by the Spaniards, transferred the economic heart of Europe from the Mediterranean to the Atlantic. Now this shift was of fundamental importance to Britain. At the beginning of the middle ages the Atlantic islands were an isolated appendage on the frontier of Europe; by the middle of the sixteenth century they lay near the centre of the most dynamic trading economy the continent had ever seen. But the transformation was a long, slow process, and its genesis must be sought in the fourteenth and fifteenth centuries, when the dominance of Venice and Genoa within the European economy still seemed unshakeable.

Ever since the Crusades had opened up the eastern Mediterranean to Christian shipping in the twelfth century, Italian galleys had sailed to Egypt and to Syria. There they loaded the silks and spices brought from the Orient either by ship to the Red Sea or by camel train to the Levant coast. Before long, the Italians also began to trade extensively in the Black Sea, this time picking up caviar, grain and, above all, slaves; and these valuable cargoes were shipped not only to Italy, but also to North Africa, to the Iberian peninsula, and even further afield to England and the Netherlands. By the fifteenth century, Italian galleys connected all the major ports of the Mediterranean and the western Atlantic in an elaborate spider's web of trade.

At first, most of the city ports of Italy participated – Amalfi, Pisa, Genoa, Venice. But before long the first two were frozen out; then Genoese trade was confined largely to the Black Sea; and eventually almost all of Europe's trade with the Near East was handled by Venice. The queen of the Adriatic became the largest city in Europe (with perhaps 120,000 inhabitants in 1400) and also one of the richest. Her annual income surpassed that of most other European states; her wealth and splendour were remarked upon by every visitor. When Philippe de Commynes, a French chronicler, passed through in 1494 he found Venice 'the most magnificent city I have ever seen'. The tapestries, marbles, palaces and conspicuous wealth simply took his breath away.[4]

But the splendour of medieval Venice rested upon foundations that were both slender and insecure. Slender, because at the heart of her prosperity lay the profits derived from importing and distributing Asiatic spices. If ever Venice lost her monopoly of this trade, her profits would necessarily be slashed. Insecure, because if ever Venice were denied access to the ports of the eastern Mediterranean, her entire spice trade would be destroyed. In the later fifteenth century, both these weaknesses were revealed and the prosperity of Venice was severely damaged.

12.3. Engraving of Venice showing the busy seafront

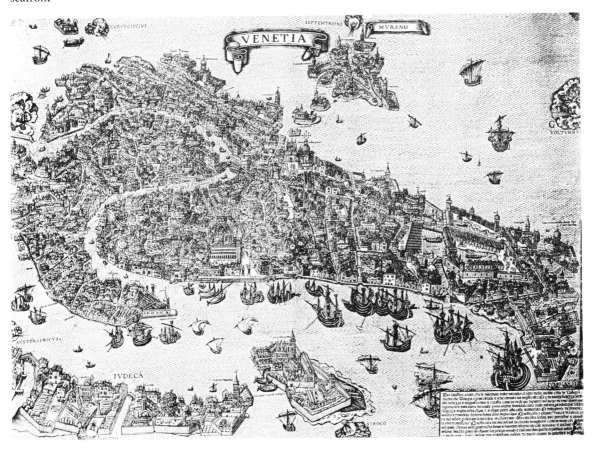

The Ottoman Turks first appear in history in the thirteenth century, as a minor tribe of warriors fighting against the Christian outposts in Anatolia. In the 1350s they crossed into Europe, taking as their capital Adrianople, which they renamed Edirne. In 1381 they defeated the Serbs and Bulgars at the battle of Kossovo, and occupied most of the Balkans. In 1453 the Turks captured, after a long siege, the capital of the Byzantine empire, Constantinople, which they renamed Istanbul. With it came the shipyards which allowed the Ottomans to create a powerful fleet. The Italian colonies and trading posts in the Black Sea and the Aegean were now doomed: one by one, the Turkish navy forced them to surrender until, by 1480, virtually none were left. In that year, the Turks carried their Holy War against Europe to Italy itself, capturing the southern port of Otranto and holding it for an entire year. Venice responded to this challenge energetically. From 1463 until 1478, and again from 1499 to 1503, the warships and troops of the republic tried to check the Turks. But in vain: in time, all her positions in Greece and the islands were lost.

As Venice staggered under the Turkish onslaught in the east, the Portuguese in the west were beginning to explore a different frontier. The key figure in this process was Prince Henry of Portugal, known since the nineteenth century as 'Henry the Navigator'. Born in 1394, the younger son of King John I, Henry at first took part in Portugal's crusade against Islam, helping to capture the town of Ceuta just across the Straits of Gibraltar in the year 1415. Although he later led another army unsuccessfully against Tangier in 1437, most of his energies and almost all of his resources were devoted to colonising the Atlantic islands, Madeira and the Azores, and making a profit from them.

In this he was remarkably successful. Sugar cane was introduced to Madeira in 1420, and within six years Madeiran sugar was being exported everywhere. Before long, annual production topped 1,000 tons, and the formerly uninhabited island was full of plantations run by slave labour. The slaves came from Africa, for Prince Henry financed exploration southwards as well as westwards. At first his tiny ships found only endless beaches. But in 1435, for the first time, footsteps were found in the sand; in 1436 some Africans were seen on the shore; and in 1440 some were captured. From Arguim in the Gambia, where the Portuguese built a small fort, trade began to flourish: the produce of Portugal and her Atlantic islands was exchanged for slaves. In 1445 the first auction of black slaves, some 250 in number, was held at Prince Henry's headquarters.[5]

What precisely had caused the prince to send his ships 1,500 miles south of the Algarve? Unfortunately, he never committed his reasons to paper; but his court historian did. Gomes Eannes de Azurara, in his *Chronicle of Guinea*, suggested that Henry was led not so much by the lure of profit as by the desire to undermine the power of Islam. According to Azurara, the prince hoped to make contact (and, if possible, an alliance) with other enemies of the Muslims further south.[6] But none were found. The blacks of the Gambia and beyond had heard neither of Mohammed nor of Christ, so crusading almost inevitably gave way to commerce.

In fact, Azurara ended his *Chronicle of Guinea* with the events of the year 1448 on a note of disgust because, in his own words:

> After that date, things were not conducted with the same vigour and fortitude as before; from this year onwards, the affairs of those parts were always managed more through treaties and trading agreements than by endurance and force of arms.[7]

But these regrets were by no means shared by everyone. The profits gained by selling black slaves – in Portugal, in the Azores and Madeira, even in England – soon attracted foreign capital, especially from Genoa. Portugal had long been a favourite with Genoese investors and entrepreneurs. Since the year 1317, the Admiral of Portugal had always been a Genoese, and he was paid by the crown to maintain a team of twenty Italian pilots and naval experts in Lisbon. The Portuguese capital had a vigorous Genoese community, with its own consul. Its members traded on their own behalf, of course, but they also carried out exploration and even colonisation on behalf of the crown. The so-called 'Catalan Atlas' of 1375 shows the Genoese flag floating over one of the Canary Islands, because it was discovered by Lanzarotto Malocello of Genoa. In his honour, the island is still called Lanzarote.

The Italians were already familiar with colonial enterprise. From their outposts around the Black Sea and the Levant, they had mastered the most effective methods of running overseas colonies, usually with the aid of slave labour, and had built up a network for selling the goods thus produced to maximum advantage. The wine, sugar and dyes produced by Italian entrepreneurs on the Atlantic islands were all crops whose profitability had previously been demonstrated in the colonies of the Aegean and the Black Sea.[8]

The Italians also brought with them formidable cartographic skills. The map of 1375 already shows familiarity not only with the Mediterranean and North Atlantic coasts, but also with West Africa's shores. Before long, more details could be added. Andrea Bianco's map of 1448 shows the African coasts as far as Senegal. Forty years later, in Henry Martellus's world map of 1489, the Cape of Good Hope is shown and the passage to India lies open. The extraordinary precision of all the coastlines on the surviving maps reflects the fact

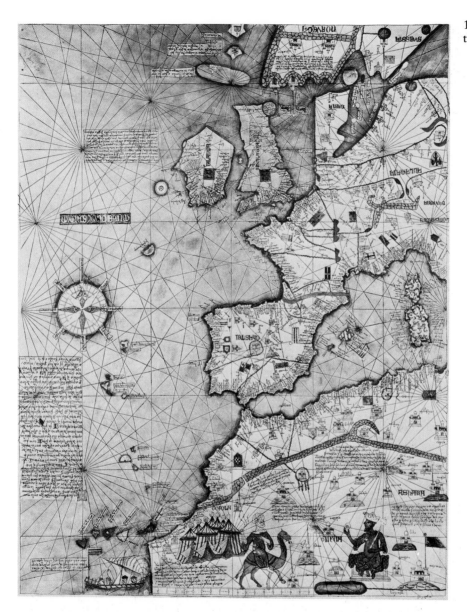

12.4a. Western half of the Catalan Atlas, 1375

that the explorers' ships hugged the shore as they proceeded along the coast of Africa. They must have sailed by day and anchored by night.

There were sound reasons for this. Above all, these vessels were surprisingly small: few sailing ships in the fifteenth century were larger than 100 tons. Vasco da Gama discovered the sea route to India with ships that measured only 70 feet from stem to stern. The ships of the pioneers were round as well as small, often little more than twice as long as they were broad, with two masts. The classic vessel of

12.4b. Eastern half of the Catalan Atlas, 1375

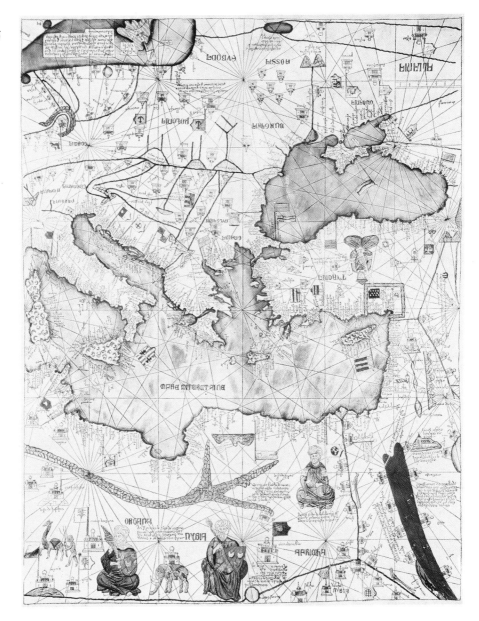

discovery, the *caravel*, was lateen-rigged, single-decked, and unarmed. Only later were a fo'c's'le and tiered upper decks at the stern added. The sixteenth century galleons or *carracks*, as these larger vessels were known, were square-rigged, and bristled with guns on two, three and even four decks. Weighing up to 2,000 tons, they were the largest wooden ships ever built. They were not constructed to hug the coast, because their draught was too deep, but rather to strike out onto the high seas. For the mariners of Europe had now discovered ways of

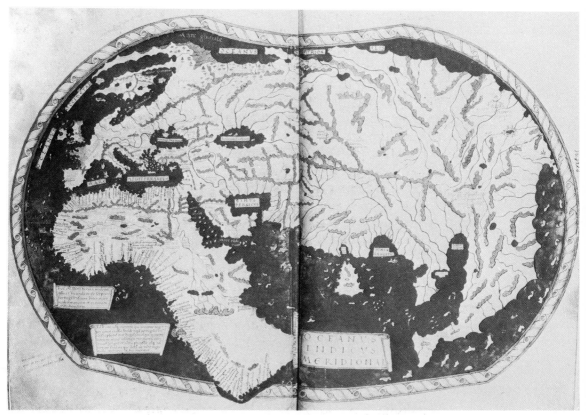

12.5. The Martellus
Map: *Mappa Mundi*

12.6. Medieval ship-
building

finding their position at sea when no land was to be seen.[9]

The compass had become familiar to European pilots by the mid-thirteenth century. But although it could establish a ship's direction, the compass could not show the distance travelled. For this, navigators came to rely on complex instruments such as the quadrant. First one gazed through it towards the sun at midday or towards the stars at night. Their precise angle above the horizon was then read off against the calibrations on the instrument; and these, in theory, revealed the ship's exact position. Star charts might also be helpful.[10]

But experience still mattered as much as instruments. After all, a compass was affected by magnetic variation, and a quadrant might be useless aboard a rolling ship or on a cloudy day. Some explorers, indeed, considered that navigational aids did more harm than good. The annals of European discovery are full of incompetent pilots like Mr Thomas Hood, aboard one of Queen Elizabeth's pirate vessels in 1582, who proudly boasted that he had no use for either compass or quadrant. 'I give not a fart for all their cosmography,' he claimed, 'for I can tell more than all the cosmographers in the world.' Not surprisingly, he guided his ship to the River Plate instead of to China; and there one of the boats steered into the coast and was wrecked, delivering her crew to the native Indians who enslaved the fittest and ate the rest.[11]

However, Thomas Hood belonged to a dying breed. By his day few still disputed the advantages of charts and compasses. It was above all thanks to their instruments that the Portuguese and Italian captains employed by Henry the Navigator made such rapid progress. In the 1450s the Cape Verde islands were discovered, and gold was found in the Gambia, so that the Lisbon mint was able to issue gold coins from 1457. Despite Prince Henry's death in 1460, trade with these areas continued to grow, and new coastal regions were brought into the Portuguese trading network. In 1481 a new fort was built at São Jorge da Minha – St George of the Mine – so called because it was near to the gold mines of the upper Niger. About the same time, the islands of São Thomé and Principe, in the Bight of Benin, were colonised and made into entrepôts for slaves. The parts of Africa closest to the islands became known as 'the Slave Coast'; the great waterways of the hinterland were called 'the five slave rivers'. By the 1490s, Lisbon was receiving some 4 kilograms of gold and perhaps 3,000 slaves every year from West Africa. There were also large quantities of ivory, artwork, pepper and other products of the area, all of them resold at enormous profit. Yet the trade of Guinea was soon eclipsed, both in volume and in value, by another: the trade with India.[12]

As Henry the Navigator's ships pressed ever southwards, hopes began to rise that a direct searoute to India might be found, a way of

12.7. Early navigation instruments in use

bringing the silks and spices of the Orient, and the profits of handling them, to Lisbon instead of to Venice. So exploration continued south of the Bight of Benin, even though the coasts were once again barren and apparently deserted. Finally, in 1488, a ship piloted by Bartolomeu Dias rounded the Cape of Good Hope and entered the Indian Ocean. On the basis of his observations, and those of other explorers sent overland to East Africa and Persia, the Portuguese worked out how it might be possible to sail directly from Europe to the pepper groves of south India. In 1497 Vasco da Gama led a small armed flotilla from the Tagus; in March 1498 he reached Mozambique in east Africa and, thanks to the monsoon, he crossed the Indian Ocean to the pepper capital of Calicut in just three weeks. Within a year he was back with his precious cargo in Lisbon.

There have been many contrary claims concerning the significance of Vasco's voyage. It used to be thought that the arrival of the Portuguese in India caused the immediate and irreversible collapse of the Venetian spice trade, and indeed of the entire Venetian economy.

12.8. The waterfront at Lisbon

There is certainly some evidence to support this view. One of the republic's historians wrote in 1509:

> The news [of the Portuguese exploit] has been regarded here as nothing short of a catastrophe, and some of our wisest men were inclined to see it as the beginning of the decline of Venice.

But such pessimism proved premature. The city's population rose from 115,000 in 1509, the year of this despairing forecast, to 168,000 in the 1560s. The production of textiles in the city over the same period shot up from 1,310 cloths to 26,500. Even the average annual spice import rose to higher levels than ever before: 1·3 million pounds in the 1560s, as against only 1·15 million pounds in the 1490s. It was hardly an economic catastrophe![13]

The explanation of this recovery was simple. At first, to be sure, the arrival of the Portuguese caused total dislocation and panic reactions – not unlike the immediate aftermath in Europe of the oil crisis of 1973. But, in time, the market was reorganised. It was found that the Portuguese, few in numbers and operating 10,000 miles from their base, lacked the resources to control the entire trade of southern Asia. Above all, they failed to close access to the Red Sea. So Muslim traders were still able to send their rich merchandise from India to Alexandria and Beirut, where the Venetians were still waiting. The Portuguese had thus succeeded only in increasing the volume of Asian goods reaching Europe, particularly north-western Europe. It was one factor, but by no means the only factor, contributing to the shift from the Mediterranean to the Atlantic.

For the opening of the Atlantic to intercontinental trade in the fifteenth century was not the work of the Portuguese alone. It was also the result of a daring voyage made by a Genoese adventurer in Spanish service who had convinced himself that one could reach the Indies by sailing westwards from Europe.

Christopher Columbus arrived in Lisbon in the year 1477 at the age of 26. He came as the factor for a merchant of his home town, and spent ten years travelling to England, Morocco and Iceland, besides commuting between Lisbon and the Azores, on his master's business. He settled in Portugal, having married the daughter of a governor of the Azores. While at home, he read voraciously in works of cosmography and entered into correspondence with the leading geographers of his day. Always his interest was directed towards a single problem: was it possible to sail west from Lisbon and reach China? Of course the answer is 'yes', although the distance is some 16,000 miles and requires a passage through the Panama canal. But Columbus did not know that! Instead, he believed that Asia was larger than it really is; second, he thought the world was smaller than it really is. Taken together, these miscalculations suggested that eastern China was only 4,000 miles away from western Europe.

It seems an absurd error to us; and it seemed absurd to the king of Portugal, to whom Columbus tried to sell his idea in 1485. But one of the distinctive strengths of early modern Europe, and one that is today often forgotten, was its political fragmentation. In China, failure to interest the emperor in a scheme always proved fatal; in Europe, failure to interest one ruler was less serious. The determined explorer could always try elsewhere. So Columbus laid his scheme before the kings of England and France. They, too, rejected him. But in 1492 Queen Isabella of Castile decided to take the risk; she provided enough money for Columbus to hire three small ships and their crews for a westward journey to China.[14]

12.9. Christopher Columbus

12.10. The landfall of
Christopher Columbus
in the New World

At first, it seemed that Columbus had got his sums right after all,
4,000 miles west of Lisbon he did find land; and, to his dying day, he
believed he had discovered parts of Asia. But others soon realised that
the lands belonged to a vast new continent, which they called
America. Within a generation, Spanish conquerors had claimed for

their ruler an area that was eight times the size of Spain and contained almost one-fifth of the world's population. The wealth of the new colonies helped to make Spain great, and placed her at the centre of affairs. As a Spanish scholar wrote triumphantly in the year 1524: 'Formerly we were at the end of the world, but now we are right in the middle of it.'[15]

What was true for Spain in 1524 was soon to prove true for Britain. The shift to the Atlantic brought the economic heart of the continent to Britain's shores. The islands had an ample supply of ships, sailors and goods for trade; they also now possessed an advantageous geographical position. It would not be long before these assets were turned to advantage. The 'principall navigations' of the English, Scots and Irish were about to commence.

Further Reading

J.J. Murray, *Antwerp in the Age of Plantin and Breughel* (Newton Abbot, 1972); J.H. Parry, *The Age of Reconnaissance. Discovery, Exploration and Settlement 1450–1650* (London, 1973); D.B. Quinn, *England and the Discovery of America 1481–1620* (New York, 1974); G.V. Scammell, *The World Encompassed. The First European Maritime Empires c. 800–1650* (London, 1981); E.G.R. Taylor, *The Haven-Finding Art. A History of Navigation from Odysseus to Captain Cook* (London, 1956); D. O'Sullivan, *The Age of Discovery 1400–1550* (London, 1984).

Notes

1. The Outer Edge of the Earth *W.L. Warren*

1. Bibliothèque Nationale, Paris MS. Lat. 8878, ff. 45v, 46.
2. He was commenting on Ezekiel V.5: 'Thus saith the Lord God: this is Jerusalem: I have set it in the midst of the nations and countries that are round about her.' On the Jerusalem-centred *mappa mundi* see R.W. Southern, *The Making of the Middle Ages* (London, 1953), pp. 69ff., and M.T. Clanchy, *England and its Rulers, 1066–1272* (London, 1983), pp. 20ff.
3. Clanchy, op. cit., pp. 22–9.
4. On the changing attitudes in western Christendom which made the crusading idea possible, see S. Runciman, *A History of the Crusades* (3 vols, Cambridge, 1951–4), vol. I, books I and II; Southern, op. cit., especially pp. 49–55; and on the nature and launching of the crusades, L. and J. Riley-Smith, *The Crusades: Idea and Reality, 1095–1274* (Documents of Medieval History 4, London, 1981).
5. Anna Comnena, *Alexiad*, ed. B. Leib (3 vols, Paris, 1937–45), e.g. II 220ff., III 122–4; see also A. Bryer, 'The first encounter with the West, AD1050–1204', in *Byzantium: an Introduction*, ed. P. Whitting (Oxford, 1971), pp. 85–110.
6. Cf. R.W. Southern, *Western Society and the Church in the Middle Ages* (London, 1970), pp. 34ff., and *The Making of the Middle Ages*, pp. 135–6.
7. G. Duby, *The Early Growth of the European Economy* (London, 1974), pp. 6–11.
8. Significantly, agricultural productivity in northern Italy came to depend on an elaborate irrigation system, see Lynn White, 'The expansion of technology, 500–1500', in *The Fontana Economic History of Europe: The Middle Ages*, ed. C.M. Cipolla (London, 1972), p. 154.
9. Duby, op. cit., pp. 11–13, and J.C. Russell, 'Population in Europe, 500–1500', in *The Fontana Economic History of Europe: The Middle Ages*, ch. 1.
10. Duby, op. cit., pp. 129–39.

11. Raoul Glaber, *Francorum Historia*, ed. M. Prou (Paris, 1886), Bk III, ch. 4, and Bk IV, ch. 6.

12. On the clearance of the forest and the 'internal colonisation' of Europe, see C.T. Smith, *An Historical Geography of Western Europe before 1800* (London, 1967), pp. 163–71.

13. Cf. F. Heer, *The Medieval World* (London, 1961), pp. 40–3.

14. *Gesta Episcoporum Cameracensium*, III, ch. 52, *Monumenta Germaniae Historica, Scriptores*, vii. 485–6; see also Duby, op. cit., pp. 164ff.

15. On this see D.C. Douglas, *The Norman Achievement, 1050–1100* (London, 1969), ch. 5, and I.S. Robinson, 'Gregory VII and the Soldiers of Christ', *History*, LVIII (1973), pp. 169–92.

16. For the technical factors in the development of heavy cavalry, see Lynn White, *Medieval Technology and Social Change* (Oxford, 1962), ch. 1.

17. Quoted by Anna Comnena, *Alexiad*, XIII, c.8.

18. For the battle at Civitate and a comparison with Hastings, see Douglas, op. cit., ch. 4, and J.J. Cooper, *The Normans in the South, 1016–1130* (London, 1967), ch. 7.

19. For these developments in Normandy, see R.H.C. Davis, *The Normans and their Myth* (London, 1976), ch. 1, and D. Bates, *Normandy before 1066* (London, 1982), part two. The archbishops were Lanfranc (1070–89) and Anselm (1093–1109); both had previously been abbots at the abbey of Bec.

20. Southern, op. cit., pp. 43–4.

21. S. Potter, *Our Language* (London, 1950), pp. 29–33.

22. For an authoritative guide to the events of 1066, see D.C. Douglas, *William the Conqueror* (London, 1964), ch. 8.

23. ibid., and H.R. Loyn, *The Norman Conquest* (3rd edn, London, 1982).

24. D. Renn, *Norman Castles in Britain* (New York, 1968; London, 1973).

25. S. Potter, op. cit., pp. 35–8.

26. J.J. Cooper, op. cit., especially p. 231.

27. S. Runciman, op. cit., I, pp. 227–8.

28. T. Rowley, *The Norman Heritage, 1066–1200* (London, 1983), p. 116; and for the bitterness of the conquered, F. Barlow, *The English Church, 1066–1154* (London, 1979), pp. 10–11.

29. R.H.C. Davis, op. cit., pp. 114ff.

30. William of Malmesbury, *Gesta Regum Anglorum*, ed. W. Stubbs, (Rolls Series, 1887–9), II, p. 334.

2.   The New Europeans   *Anne Duggan*

1. Quoted by J.W. Baldwin, 'Masters at Paris from 1179–1215: A Social Perspective' in R.L. Benson and G. Constable (eds), *Renaissance and Renewal in the Twelfth Century* (Cambridge, Mass., 1982), p. 140.

2. Marie-Thérèse d'Alverny, 'Translations and Translators' in Benson *et al.*, op. cit., pp. 421–62.

3. John of Salisbury, *The Metalogicon*, trans. D.D. McGarry (Berkeley, Calif., 1962), pp. 96–9.
4. Baldwin, op. cit., pp. 148–50.
5. A.C. Crombie, *Robert Grosseteste and the Origins of Experimental Science 1100–1700* (Oxford, 1953), p. 43.
6. C. Duggan, *Twelfth-Century Decretal Collections and their import-ance in English history* (London, 1963), especially pp. 19–23; see also E. Friedberg (ed.), *Corpus Iuris Canonici*, 2 vols (Leipzig, 1879–81).
7. Geoffrey of Monmouth, *Historia Regum Britanniae*, ed. Jacob Hammer (Medieval Academy of America no. 57, Cambridge, Mass., 1951); *Giraldi Cambrensis Opera*, 8 vols, eds J.S. Brewer, J.F. Dimock and G.F. Warner (Rolls Series 21, London, 1861–91); William of Malmes-bury, *Historia Novella*, ed. K.R. Potter (Nelson's Medieval Texts, 1955); William of Newburgh, *Historia Rerum Anglicarum*, ed. R.G. Howlett, *Chronicles of the Reigns of Stephen, Henry II and Richard I*, 2 vols (Rolls Series 82, London, 1884–5); *Chronica Magistri Rogeri de Hovedene*, 4 vols, ed. William Stubbs (Rolls Series 51, London, 1868–71); *Radulphi de Diceto decani Lundoniensis Opera Historica*, 2 vols, ed. William Stubbs (Rolls Series 68, London, 1876); William FitzStephen, *Vita Beati Thomae Martyris, Materials for the History of Thomas Becket*, eds J.C. Robertson and J.B. Sheppard, 7 vols (Rolls Series 67, London, 1875–85), III, pp. 1–154.
8. C. Duggan, 'Bishop John and Archdeacon Richard of Poitiers: Their roles in the Becket dispute and its aftermath' in *Canon Law in Medieval England* (Variorum Reprints, 1982), cap. XIII.
9. R.W. Southern, 'The Schools of Paris and the School of Chartres' in Benson *et al.*, op. cit., pp. 134–5; *Materials for the History of Thomas Becket*, op. cit., III, pp. 523–31: eighteen of the twenty-two listed are masters.
10. J. Baldwin, op. cit., pp. 155–7.
11. D.E.R. Watt, *A Biographical Dictionary of Scottish Graduates before 1410* (Oxford, 1979).
12. *Pipe Roll 31 Henry I*, and *Pipe Rolls 2–4 Henry II*, ed. J. Hunter (Record Commission, London, 1833–4) and reissued by the Pipe Roll Society, 1929 and 1930.
13. P.H. Brieger, *English Art 1216–1307* (Oxford, 1957), p. 25; see also John Harvey, 'The Development of Architecture' in *The Flowering of the Middle Ages*, ed. Joan Evans (London, 1966), pp. 81–132.
14. John of Salisbury, *Historia Pontificalis*, ed. and trans. Marjorie Chibnall (London, 1956), pp. 79–80.
15. C.N.L. Brooke, *The Twelfth Century Renaissance* (London, 1969), p. 149 and Plates 117 and 118.
16. C.N.L. Brooke, op. cit., p. 149; see also Ursula Nilgen, 'Thomas Becket as a Patron of the Arts: The Wall Painting of St Anselm's Chapel at Canterbury Cathedral', *Art History* 3 (1980), pp. 357–74 and Plates 1 and 2.

3. Magna Carta and Royal Government *John Gillingham*

1. J.C. Holt, *Magna Carta* (Cambridge, 1965) is now the standard work on the charter in its historical setting. Important appendices provide the text of Magna Carta (with an English translation) and some of the related documents. Other accessible translations include J.C. Dickinson, *The Great Charter* (Historical Association, 1955) and Appendix B to W.L. Warren, *King John* (London, 1961).

2. M.T. Clanchy, *England and its Rulers, 1066–1272* (London, 1983), p. 198.

3. See, for example, A. Pallister, *Magna Carta: The Heritage of Liberty* (Oxford, 1971).

4. For more than twenty years the study of patronage has been a fashionable subject among medievalists – and rightly so. Its fundamental importance for the politics of the period was elegantly sketched out by R.W. Southern, 'The Place of Henry I in English History', *Proceedings of the British Academy* (1962), reprinted in his *Medieval Humanism and Other Studies* (Oxford, 1970).

5. Walter Map, *De Nugis Curialium: Courtiers' Trifles*, ed. and trans. M.R. James, reissued by C.N.L. Brooke and R.A.B. Mynors (Oxford, 1983).

6. The abundance of record evidence for John's reign means that this is the earliest rebellion which it is possible to study in depth. The opportunity was grasped, in masterful fashion, by J.C. Holt, *The Northerners* (Oxford, 1961).

7. J.C. Holt, op. cit., p. 34.

8. Most modern historians treat John much more sympathetically than I do, emphasising in particular his supposed qualities as an administrator, e.g. D.M. Stenton, 'King John and the Courts of Justice', *Proceedings of the British Academy* (1958); reprinted in her *English Justice Between the Norman Conquest and the Great Charter* (London, 1965); W.L. Warren, op. cit.; J.C. Holt, *King John* (Historical Association, 1963).

9. J. Le Patourel, 'The Plantagenet Dominions', *History*, L (1965).

10. See J. Gillingham, *The Angevin Empire* (London, 1984), and for the contrast with Richard, J. Gillingham, *Richard the Lionheart* (London, 1978).

11. Quoted from J.C. Holt, *King John*, p. 17.

12. See J.C. Holt, *Magna Carta*, pp. 300–2 for the text of Henry I's charter.

4. War, Politics and Parliament *Chris Given-Wilson*

1. There is a massive literature on the Anglo-French and Anglo-Scottish wars of the late middle ages, but perhaps the most useful general studies are: K. Fowler, *The Age of Plantagenet and Valois* (London, 1967); E. Perroy, *The Hundred Years War* (London, 1951); J. Campbell, 'England, Scotland, and the Hundred Years War', in *Europe in the*

Later Middle Ages, (eds) J.R. Hale, J.R.L. Highfield and B. Smalley (London, 1965); and M.G.A. Vale, *War and Chivalry* (London, 1981).

2. For Richard II's foreign policy, see J.J.N. Palmer, *England, France and Christendom 1377–1399* (Woodbridge, 1972).

3. Henry VI's reign, including his foreign policy, is fully dealt with in two recent works, R.A. Griffiths, *The Reign of Henry VI* (London, 1981), and B.P. Wolffe, *Henry VI* (London, 1981).

4. Philippe de Mézières, for example, writing about 1390, declared that 'everyone knows that in all Christian and heathen countries there are three estates, that is the clergy, the nobles, and the people' Philippe de Mézières, *Le Songe de Vieil Pelerin*, ed. G.W. Coopland (Cambridge, 1969), I, p. 526.

5. For Henry's settlement in Normandy see C.T. Allmand, *Lancastrian Normandy 1415–1450* (London, 1983) and A.J. Pollard, *John Talbot and the War in France 1427–53* (London, 1984).

6. On the conduct and profits of war, see M.H. Keen, *The Laws of War in the Late Middle Ages* (London, 1965): D. Hay, 'The Division of Spoils of War in Fourteenth-century England', *Transactions of the Royal Historical Society* (1954); C. Given-Wilson, 'The Ransom of Olivier du Guesclin', *Bulletin of the Institute of Historical Research* (1981).

7. Much of the historical literature on late medieval France testifies to the devastation caused by the war; a graphic account, concentrating on the Bordeaux region, is the classic study by R. Boutruche, *La Crise d'une Société: Seigneurs et Paysans du Bordelais pendant la Guerre de Cent Ans* (Paris, 1947).

8. For these kings and their ransoms see E.W.M. Balfour-Melville, *Edward III and David II* (Historical Association, 1954), and D.M. Broome, 'The Ransom of John II, King of France', *Camden Miscellany* XIV (1926).

9. The fullest description of Edward's building programme at Windsor, together with maps and illustrations, is in *The History of the King's Works*, ed. H.M. Colvin *et al.*, I–III (London, 1963).

10. Much has been written about royal armies in the middle ages; perhaps the most useful studies are M.R. Powicke, *Military Obligation in Medieval England* (Oxford, 1962), and M.C. Prestwich, *War, Politics and Finance under Edward I* (London, 1972).

11. The standard work on taxation and parliament in the thirteenth and fourteenth centuries is now G.L. Harriss, *King, Parliament and Public Finance in England to 1369* (Oxford, 1975).

12. There is a massive literature on the origins of parliament; a particularly good book is *The English Parliament in the Middle Ages*, eds R.G. Davies and J.H. Denton (Manchester, 1981), where references to other studies can be found.

13. For the lords, see J.E. Powell and K. Wallis, *The House of Lords in the Middle Ages* (London, 1968).

14. The best modern account of the events is G.A. Holmes, *The Good Parliament* (Oxford, 1975). It was a very well-documented parliament, and there are lengthy contemporary accounts of the proceedings in

Rotuli Parliamentorum (the official parliamentary record), vol. II, pp. 321–60; Thomas Walsingham's *Chronicon Angliae 1328-88*, ed. E.M. Thompson (Rolls Series, 1874), pp. 68–101; and, most valuable of all because it is an eye-witness account very probably by a member of the commons, *The Anonimalle Chronicle*, ed. V.H. Galbraith (Manchester, 1927), pp. 79–94.

15. For de la Mare, see the short biography by J.S. Roskell, 'Sir Peter de la Mare, Speaker for the Commons in Parliament in 1376 and 1377', *Nottingham Medieval Studies*, II (1958); for his outspokenness, Sir Peter was imprisoned in Nottingham Castle in October 1376; at the beginning of the new reign in June 1377 he was released, and was once more chosen by the commons to be their speaker in the parliament which met in October 1377. There is a further biography of him in J.S. Roskell, *The Commons and their Speakers in English Parliaments 1376–1523* (Manchester, 1965).

16. *Anonimalle Chronicle*, op. cit., p. 90.

17. For discussion of the king and his relations to parliament generally, see K.B. McFarlane, *The Nobility of Later Medieval England* (Oxford, 1973), especially pp. 120–1.

5.   The Triumph of Scotland   *Alexander Grant*

1. J. Le Patourel, *The Norman Empire* (Oxford, 1976), p. 67, from the Anglo-Saxon Chronicle, 1072. See also A.A.M. Duncan, *Scotland: The Making of the Kingdom* (Edinburgh, 1975), pp. 119–20.

2. For the conquests in Wales and Ireland see D. Walker, *The Norman Conquerors* (Swansea, 1977); J. Le Patourel, op. cit., pp. 61–7, 211–3, 312–4; J.G. Edwards, 'The Normans and the Welsh March', *Proceedings of the British Academy*, XLII, (1956); D.Ó Corráin, *Ireland before the Normans* (Dublin, 1972); R. Frame, *Colonial Ireland* (Dublin, 1981); and W.L. Warren, *Henry II* (London, 1973), pp. 153–69, 181–206.

3. A.A.M. Duncan, op. cit., chs. 4–6.

4. ibid., chapters 7 and 8; G.W.S. Barrow, *The Anglo-Norman Era in Scottish History* (Oxford, 1980).

5. This is reflected in the addresses to royal charters. In Malcolm IV's reign and the first part of William I's, it was fairly common for the king to address charters to 'all his good men, French [those of Norman, Breton or Flemish origin], English [those from Lothian] and Scots'; but from about 1180 this racial form of address disappears, and the standard form becomes 'all good men of his whole land'. See *Regesta Regum Scottorum*: I, *The Acts of Malcolm IV*, ed. G.W.S. Barrow (Edinburgh, 1960); II, *The Acts of William I*, ed. G.W.S. Barrow with W.W. Scott (Edinburgh, 1971).

6. For the wealth of late thirteenth century Scotland, see N.J. Mayhew, 'Money in thirteenth century Scotland', in *Coinage in Medieval*

Scotland, ed. D. Metcalf (British Archaeological Reports, 45, 1977).

7. All the documents relating to the Great Cause are printed and analysed in E.L.G. Stones and G.G. Simpson, *Edward I and the Throne of Scotland* (Glasgow, 1979).

8. From a 'diary' of Edward I's 1296 campaign, printed in *A Source Book of Scottish History*, ed. W.C. Dickinson *et al.* (Edinburgh, 1958), I, p. 10.

9. Robert I, who took over the Scottish throne in 1306, was the grandson of Robert Bruce of Annandale, John Balliol's main rival in the 1291–2 competition for the throne. His career is studied in G.W.S. Barrow, *Robert Bruce and the Community of the Realm in Scotland* (2nd edition Edinburgh, 1976).

10. The main clauses are translated in *Source Book of Scottish History*, I, pp. 160–2; see also *The Acts of the Parliament of Scotland*, I, ed. C. Innes (Edinburgh, 1844), pp. 484–7.

11. R.R. Davies, 'Colonial Wales' in *Past and Present*, 65 (1974); R.R. Davies, *Lordship and Society in the March of Wales, 1282-1400* (Oxford, 1978), chs. 1–4.

12. ibid., pp. 26–33.

13. SIGILLVM SCOCIE DEPVTATVM REGIMINI REGNI; ANDREA SCOTIS DVX ESTO COMPATRIOTIS. See G.W.S. Barrow, op. cit., p. 24.

14. The Declaration of Arbroath has been printed in many places, including *The Acts of the Parliaments of Scotland*, I, pp. 474–5, and *Source Book of Scottish History*, I, pp. 151–8. I have used A.A.M. Duncan's translation in *The Nation of the Scots and the Declaration of Arbroath* (Historical Association, 1970), pp. 34–7.

15. G.W.S. Barrow, op. cit., pp. 142–5, interpreted in the light of J.A. Keegan, *The Face of Battle* (London, 1976), chs. 1 and 2, which is fundamental to any study of medieval warfare.

16. G. Donaldson, *Scottish Kings* (London, 1967), p. 62.

17. Notably by Dr Jenny Wormald (formerly Brown): J.M. Brown, 'Taming the Magnates' in *The Scottish Nation*, ed. G. Menzies (London, 1972), reprinted in *Essays on the Nobility of Medieval Scotland*, ed. K.J. Stringer (Edinburgh, 1985); J.M. Brown, 'The Exercise of Power' in *Scottish Society in the Fifteenth Century*, ed. J.M. Brown (London, 1977); J. Wormald, *Court, Kirk and Community: Scotland 1470–1625* (London, 1981), ch. 1. See also N.A.T. Macdougall, 'The Sources: a reappraisal of the Legend' in *Scottish Society in the Fifteenth Century*, and *James III: A Political Study* (Edinburgh, 1982). The new approach is also to be found in A.A.M. Duncan's revision of W.C. Dickinson, *Scotland from Earliest Times to 1603* (Oxford, 1977), and in ch. 7 of A. Grant, *Independence and Nationhood: Scotland 1306–1469* (London, 1984).

18. The figures derive from standard political histories of both countries, and from *The Scots Peerage*, ed. J.B. Paul (Edinburgh, 1904–14) and *The Complete Peerage*, ed. G.E. Cockayne *et al.* (London, 1910–59).

19. From an anonymous contemporary chronicle, printed in *The Asloan Manuscript*, ed. W.A. Craigie, I, (Scottish Text Society, 1923), p. 239.
20. ibid., p. 238.
21. The points in this and the following paragraphs are developed in A. Grant, *Independence and Nationhood*, chs. 5 and 6.
22. A.I. Dunlop, *The Life and Times of James Kennedy, Bishop of St Andrews* (Edinburgh, 1950), p. 2.
23. This is argued at length in A. Grant, 'Crown and Politics in late Medieval Britain' which is to be published in a collection of essays on Scottish and English history, edited by J. Campbell and M. Hurst.
24. The only exception to this is in the reign of James III, who did in the end manage to alienate much of the normal support for the crown, and paid the penalty in 1488 when he was killed. See N.A.T. Macdougall, *James III*.
25. My view of late medieval English history has been strongly influenced by R.L. Storey, *The End of the House of Lancaster* (London, 1966). See also N. Fryde, *The Tyranny and Fall of Edward II* (Cambridge, 1979); A. Tuck, *Richard II and the English Nobility* (London, 1973); R.A. Griffiths, *The Reign of King Henry VI* (London, 1981); C. Ross, *Edward IV* (London, 1974) and *Richard III* (London, 1981).
26. *The Acts of the Parliaments of Scotland*, I, pp. 504, 509, 556; A.A.M. Duncan, *James I* (University of Glasgow, Scottish History Department, occasional papers, no. 1, 1976).

6. Working the Land *David Carpenter*

1. Information about Willingham comes from material collected by Christopher Lewis for the forthcoming volume IX of the *Victoria County History* for Cambridgeshire.
2. For Broughton, see *Victoria County History Oxfordshire*, vol. IX, p. 85.
3. For manor houses, see M. Wood, *The English Mediaeval House* (London, 1965).
4. Wood, op. cit., pp. 215–6.
5. For Cuxham, see P.D.A. Harvey, *A Medieval Oxfordshire Village: Cuxham 1240–1400* (Oxford, 1965), p. 25; for East Witton, see C.H. Knowles, *Landscape History* (Historical Association, 1983), p. 13; for Laxton, see C.S. and C.S. Orwin, *The Open Fields* (Oxford, 1967).
6. For the Domesday entry relating to Cuxham, see *Victoria County History Oxfordshire*, vol. I, p. 419. For the size of the individual holdings, see P.D.A. Harvey, op. cit., pp. 119–121, 130.
7. For Spalding and Taunton, see J.L. Bolton, *The Medieval English Economy 1150–1500* (London, 1980), p. 57.
8. I have assumed that the bordars of Domesday Book are the equivalent of cottagers in the survey of 1279, *Victoria County History Oxfordshire*, vol. I, p. 479; *Rotuli Hundredorum*, vol. II (Record Commission, 1818),

p. 758 (the 1279 survey); see also P.D.A. Harvey, op. cit., p. 120.

9. The fullest discussion of the standard of living of the peasantry in the thirteenth century is found in J.Z. Titow, *English Rural Society 1200–1350* (London, 1969), ch. 3.

10. For the development of villeinage see R.H. Hilton, 'Freedom and Villeinage in England', *Past and Present*, XXXI (1965).

11. R.H. Hilton, 'Peasant Movements in England before 1381', *Economic History Review*, 2nd series, II (1949), p. 135.

12. J.Z. Titow, op. cit., p. 70.

13. P. Ziegler, *The Black Death* (Harmondsworth, 1970) provides a useful general account of the plague.

14. P.D.A. Harvey, op. cit., p. 136.

15. J.L. Bolton, op. cit., p. 71.

16. This is argued, for example, in R.H. Hilton, *The Decline of Serfdom in Medieval England* (London, 1969).

17. J.L. Bolton, op. cit., p. 219.

18. See R.B. Dobson (ed.), *The Peasants' Revolt of 1381* (London, 1970), pp. 164–5, 177–8, 186, 195, 207.

19. *Calendar of Inquisitions Miscellaneous*, I (HMSO, 1916), nos. 2062, 2063, 2133.

7. The Lords of the Manor *Caroline Barron*

1. For the history of Bromholm priory see *Victoria County History of Norfolk*, ed. W. Page (London, 1906), p. 359; Lilian J. Redstone (ed.), *Cellarers Account for Bromholm Priory, Norfolk 1415–1416* (Norfolk Record Society, 1944).

2. The accounts for John Paston's funeral are to be found in James Gairdner (ed.), *The Paston Letters*, 6 vols (first edn 1904, reprinted 1983), p. 637.

3. For the delays over the construction of John Paston's tomb see Norman Davis (ed.), *Paston Letters and Papers of the Fifteenth Century*, (Oxford, 1971, part I; 1976, part II), nos. 212, 228, 264, 274, 283, 295, 309, 311, 371 (hereafter cited as *Paston Letters*).

4. C.L. Kingsford (ed.), *Stonor Letters and Papers 1290–1483*, 2 volumes (Camden Society, 1919).

5. Alison Hanham (ed.), *The Cely Letters, 1472–1488* (Oxford, 1975).

6. *Paston Letters*, no. 142.

7. *Paston Letters*, no. 90.

8. This account is printed in J. Gairdner, op. cit., I, pp. 28–9.

9. Caroline Barron, 'Who were the Pastons?', *Journal of the Society of Archivists*, vol. IV (1972), pp. 530–5.

10. *Paston Letters*, no. 129.

11. *William of Worcester: Itineraries*, ed. J.H. Harvey (Oxford, 1969).

12. *Paston Letters*, no. 897.

13. John and Margaret Paston named their first two sons John in the

expectation that one would die before manhood: both in fact survived, John II to the age of 37 and John III to the age of 60.

14. *Paston Letters*, no. 380.
15. *Paston Letters*, nos. 36, 131.
16. *Paston Letters*, nos. 252–4.
17. *Paston Letters*, nos. 286, 290, 292, 298, 300, 316.
18. *Paston Letters*, no. 271.
19. *Paston Letters*, nos. 256, 264, 272.
20. *Paston Letters*, no. 201.
21. *Paston Letters*, no. 228.
22. *Paston Letters*, no. 230.
23. *Paston Letters*, nos. 125, 153.
24. *Paston Letters*, nos. 416, 417.
25. *Paston Letters*, no. 335.
26. *A Relation or rather a true account of the Island of England*, ed. C.A. Sneyd (Camden Society, 1847), p. 25.
27. *Paston Letters*, no. 446.
28. *Paston Letters*, no. 203.
29. *Paston Letters*, no. 365.
30. *Paston Letters*, no. 293.
31. *Paston Letters*, nos. 439, 407. For the careers of the three brothers, John, William II and Clement, who went to Cambridge, see A.B. Emden, *A Bibliographical Register of the University of Cambridge to 1500* (Cambridge, 1963).
32. See *Paston Letters*, I, pp. xxxv–xxxix and plates i–xii.
33. For some reason, in 1472, the Earl of Arran had borrowed the book. See *Paston Letters*, no. 352.
34. *Paston Letters*, nos. 245, 751, 755 and see A.I. Doyle, 'The work of a late fifteenth-century English scribe, William Ebesham', *Bulletin of the John Rylands Library*, XXXIX (1957).
35. *Paston Letters*, nos. 271, 285, 286, 287, 288, 291.
36. *Paston Letters*, no. 316 and I, plate vii.

8. Towns and Trade   *Richard Mackenney*

1. On the feudal environment, see G.W.S. Barrow, *Feudal Britain* (London, 1971).
2. A.C. Cawley (ed.), *The Canterbury Tales* (Everyman edn, London, 1958), pp. 1–25.
3. C. Platt, *The English Medieval Town* (London, 1979), pp. 82–91.
4. For a general account, see M.M. Postan, *The Medieval Economy and Society* (London, 1972).
5. This essay owes much to the extraordinary insights contained in E.M. Carus-Wilson, 'The first half-century of the borough of Stratford-upon-Avon', *Economic History Review*, new series 18 (1965), pp. 46–63.

6. E.M. Carus-Wilson, 'Towns and trade', in A.L. Poole (ed.), *Medieval England*, I (Oxford, 1958), p. 224.

7. G.W.S. Barrow, *Kingship and Unity: Scotland 1000–1306* (London, 1981), pp. 84-6.

8. E.M. Carus-Wilson, 'Towns and trade', op. cit., p. 237.

9. On foreign merchants, see A.A. Ruddock, *Italian Merchants in Southampton* (Southampton, 1951); P. Dollinger, *The German Hansa* (London, 1970).

10. M.M. Postan, op. cit., p. 214.

11. For a wide-ranging survey of the stannaries, see J. Hatcher, *English Tin Production and Trade before 1550* (Oxford, 1973).

12. See A.R. Bridbury, *Medieval English Cloth-Making: An Economic Survey* (London, 1983).

13. E.M. Carus-Wilson, 'Towns and trade', op. cit., p. 243.

14. ibid., p. 249, and on markets p. 241.

15. A.E. Bland, P.A. Brown and R.H. Tawney (eds), *English Economic History: Select Documents* (London, 1914), p. 123.

16. G.A. Williams, *Medieval London: From Commune to Capital* (London, 1963), p. 1.

17. A.E. Bland *et al.*, op. cit., p. 125.

18. S.L. Thrupp, 'The Guilds', in *Cambridge Economic History of Europe*, III (Cambridge, 1963), pp. 230–81; G. Unwin, *The Gilds and Companies of London* (London, 1908); J. Harvey, *Medieval Craftsmen* (London, 1975).

19. A.B. Hibbert, 'The origins of the medieval town patriciate', *Past and Present*, 3 (1953).

20. S.L. Thrupp, *The Merchant Class of Medieval London* (Michigan, 1968); D.M. Stuart, 'William Caxton: mercer, translator and master printer', *History Today*, X (1960), pp. 256–64.

21. Illustrated in C. Platt, op. cit., p. 135.

22. ibid., p. 140.

23. ibid., pp. 57–8.

24. G.A. Williams, op. cit., pp. 106–95; on the weavers see p. 174.

25. R.H. Hilton, 'Lords, burgesses and hucksters', *Past and Present*, 97 (1982), pp. 3–15.

26. C. Platt, op. cit., pp. 191–210.

27. M.F. Westlake, *The Parish Gilds of Medieval England* (London, 1919), pp. 53–5.

28. P. Ziegler, *The Black Death* (London, 1969), pp. 120–93.

9. The Church and the Love of Christ *David Carpenter*

1. D.L. Douie and H. Farmer (eds), *Magna Vita Sancti Hugonis*, vol. II (London, 1962), pp. 140–1.

2. D.L. Douie and H. Farmer, op. cit., pp. 46–7. I have formed the quotation from several passages.

3. D.L. Douie and H. Farmer, op. cit., p. 87; J.R.H. Moorman, *Church Life in England in the Thirteenth Century* (Cambridge, 1945), pp. 210–13, and also Part One for a full analysis of the parochial situation in the thirteenth century.

4. For the papacy and the reform movement, see W. Ullmann, *A Short History of the Papacy in the Middle Ages* (London, 1972), ch. 7. See also C. Duggan, 'From the Conquest to the death of John', in *The English Church and the Papacy in the Middle Ages*, ed. C.H. Lawrence (London, 1965).

5. D.L. Douie and H. Farmer, op. cit., p. 96; R.M.T. Hill (ed.), *The Rolls and Register of Bishop Oliver Sutton*, vol. III (Lincoln Record Society, 48, 1954), pp. xiii-lxxxvi; M. Gibbs and J. Lang, *Bishops and Reform 1215–72* (Oxford, 1934).

6. For rectors and their deputies, see J.R.H. Moorman, op. cit., chs. III-V.

7. D.C. Douglas and G.W. Greenaway (eds), *English Historical Documents*, vol. II (London, 1968), p. 669.

8. D.L. Douie and H. Farmer, op. cit., p. 96. For the dispute between Gregory VII and Henry IV, see W. Ullmann, op. cit., ch. 7; G. Barraclough, *The Medieval Papacy* (London, 1968), ch. 3. For Becket and Henry II, D. Knowles, *Thomas Becket* (London, 1970); W.L. Warren, *Henry II* (London, 1973), part III.

9. For the Cistercians, see D. Knowles, *The Monastic Order in England*, (Cambridge, 1963), chs. XI–XIV.

10. H.E. Butler (ed.), *The Chronicle of Jocelin of Brakelond* (London, 1949), pp. 47, 62.

11. F.M. Powicke (ed.), *The Life of Ailred of Rievaulx by Walter Daniel* (London, 1950), pp. 37, 60.

12. For the friars see D. Knowles, *The Religious Orders in England*, vol. I (Cambridge, 1948), part two.

13. The Rule of St Francis may be found, in translation, in H. Rothwell (ed.), *English Historical Documents*, vol. III (London, 1975), no. 137.

14. A.G. Little (ed.), *Fratris Thomae de Eccleston De Adventu Fratrum Minorum in Angliam* (Manchester, 1951), pp. xxiv, 102.

15. The following discussion relies heavily on G. Leff, *Heresy in the Later Middle Ages*, 2 vols (Manchester, 1967).

16. For the Waldensians see M.D. Lambert, *Medieval Heresy* (London, 1977), ch. 6.

17. For Wycliffe's ideas, see Leff, op. cit., vol. II, ch. vii.

18. A.R. Myers (ed.), *English Historical Documents*, vol. IV (London, 1969), p. 838.

19. J.S. Brewer (ed.), *Monumenta Franciscana* (Rolls Series, 1858), pp. 606, 591.

20. For Wycliffe's following, see K.B. McFarlane, *John Wycliffe and the Beginnings of English Nonconformity* (London, 1952), and *Lancastrian Kings and Lollard Knights* (Oxford, 1972); J.A.F. Thomson, *The Later Lollards* (Oxford, 1965).

21. M. Aston, 'Lollardy and Sedition', *Past and Present*, 17 (1960).

10. The King's Peace *John Post*

1. J.C. Holt, *Robin Hood* (London, 1982).
2. R.R. Davies, 'The survival of the bloodfeud in medieval Wales', *History*, LIV (1969), pp. 338–57; J. Wormald, 'Bloodfeud, kindred, and government in early modern Scotland', *Past and Present*, 87 (1980), pp. 54–97.
3. J.B. Post, 'Local jurisdictions and judgment of death in later medieval England', *Criminal Justice History*, IV (1983), pp. 1–21.
4. J.S. Cockburn, *A History of English Assizes 1558–1714* (Cambridge, 1972), ch. 1.
5. A. Harding, 'The origins and early history of the keeper of the peace', *Transactions of the Royal Historical Society*, 5th series, X (1960), pp. 85–109.
6. F.R.H. Du Boulay, *An Age of Ambition: English Society in the Late Middle Ages* (London, 1970), plate 6.
7. M.T. Clanchy, *From Memory to Written Record: England 1066–1307* (London, 1979), pp. 74–6 and passim.
8. M.T. Clanchy, 'Highway robbery and trial by battle in the Hampshire eyre of 1249', in *Medieval Legal Records edited in memory of C.A.F. Meekings*, ed. R.F. Hunnisett and J.B. Post (London, 1978).
9. M.M. Crow and C.C. Olson (eds), *Chaucer Life-Records* (Oxford, 1966), ch. 22.
10. N.D. Hurnard, 'The jury of presentment and the assize of Clarendon', *English Historical Review*, LVI (1941).
11. See the essay by P.R. Hyams in M.S. Arnold *et al.* (eds), *On the Laws and Customs of England: Essays in Honor of Samuel E. Thorne* (Chapel Hill, 1981).
12. Examples in J.M. Kaye (ed.), *Placita Corone* (Selden Society, Supplementary Series, 4, 1966).
13. S.F.C. Milsom, *Historical Foundations of the Common Law* (London, 1969), ch. 14.
14. A.R. Myers (ed.), *English Historical Documents 1327–1485* (London, 1969), no. 723.
15. J.B. Post, 'Courts, councils and arbitrators in the Ladbroke manor dispute, 1382–1400', in R.F. Hunnisett and J.B. Post, op. cit.
16. J.B. Post, 'Ravishment of women and the statutes of Westminster', in J.H. Baker (ed.), *Legal Records and the Historian* (Royal Historical Society, Studies in History, 1978).
17. J.B. Post, 'Sir Thomas West and the statute of rapes, 1382', *Bulletin of the Institute of Historical Research*, LIII (1980), pp. 24–30.
18. J.B. Post, 'A fifteenth-century customary of the Southwark stews', *Journal of the Society of Archivists*, 7 (1977), p. 418.

11. The Written Word *M.T. Clanchy*

1. H. Jenkinson (ed.), *Domesday Book Re-bound* (London, 1954), plate 1.
2. D. Whitelock (ed.), *The Anglo-Saxon Chronicle* (London, 1961), pp. 161–2.
3. G. Constable (ed.), *The Letters of Peter the Venerable*, vol. I (Cambridge, Mass., 1967), p. 38.
4. M.T. Clanchy, *From Memory to Written Record* (London, 1979), p. 89.
5. Durham, Dean and Chapter Archives, 4.7. Spec. 9a.
6. C. Johnson (ed.), *Dialogus de Scaccario* (London, 1950), p. 26.
7. S.E. Thorne (ed.), *De Legibus*, vol. II (Cambridge, Mass., 1968), p. 22.
8. T. Wright (ed.), *Political Songs of England* (Camden Society, 1st series, vol. VI, 1839), p. 151.
9. M.T. Clanchy, *England and Its Rulers* (London and Oxford, 1983), p. 143.
10. F.W. Robinson (ed.), *The Complete Works of Geoffrey Chaucer*, 2nd edn (Oxford, 1966), p. 161.
11. E.G. Stanley (ed.), (London, 1960).
12. R.B. Dobson (ed.), *The Peasants Revolt of 1381* (London, 1970), p. 381.
13. C.E. Wright, *English Vernacular Hands* (Oxford, 1960), plate 22.

12. Europe and the Wider World *Geoffrey Parker*

1. R. Hakluyt, *The principall navigations, voiages and discoveries of the English nation* (1st edn, London, 1589), sig. *2v.
2. See the trenchant comments on this theme in D.B. Quinn and A.N. Ryan, *England's Sea-Empire 1558–1640* (London, 1983).
3. There is a lively description of early modern Antwerp by J.J. Murray, *Antwerp in the Age of Plantin and Breughel* (Newton Abbot, 1972).
4. Quoted in F.C. Lane, *Venice: a Maritime Republic* (Baltimore, 1973), p. 237.
5. See the description in C.R. Beazley and E. Prestage (eds), *The chronicle of the discovery and conquest of Guinea written by Gomes Eannes de Azurara*, vol. I. (Hakluyt Society, XCV, London, 1896), ch. 25.
6. ibid., ch. 7.
7. ibid., vol. II (Hakluyt Society, C, London, 1899), ch. 96. There is an excellent brief study of the prince and his chronicler by P.E. Russell, *Prince Henry the Navigator* (London, 1960).
8. On the role of the Italians in Iberian expansion see C. Verlinden, *The Beginnings of Modern Colonization* (Ithaca, 1970), chs 1, 2 and 6.
9. On the Portuguese and their carracks, see the many essays of C.R. Boxer collected in *From Lisbon to Goa, 1500–1750. Studies in Portuguese Maritime Enterprise* (London, 1984).

10. The best guide to all this is still E.G.R. Taylor, *The Haven-finding Art. A History of Navigation from Odysseus to Captain Cook* (London, 1956).

11. Details from E.G.R. Taylor (ed.), *The troublesome voyage of Captain Edward Fenton 1582–3. Narratives and documents* (Hakluyt Society, 2nd series, CXIII, London, 1959); and E.S. Donno (ed.), *An Elizabethan in 1582: the diary of Richard Madox, Fellow of All Souls* (Hakluyt Society, 2nd series, CXLVII, London 1976), especially p. 151.

12. See for further detail, J. Vogt, *Portuguese Rule on the Gold Coast 1469–1682* (Athens, Georgia, 1979) and A.F.C. Ryder, *Benin and the Europeans, 1485–1897* (London, 1969).

13. Quotation and details from F.C. Lane, *Venice and History* (Baltimore, 1966), chs 1 and 2.

14. There is much new material in J. Heers, *Christophe Colomb* (Paris, 1981).

15. Memorial of Hernan Perez de Oliva of Cordoba quoted in J.H. Elliott, *The Old World and the New 1492–1650* (Cambridge, 1970), p. 73.

Notes on Contributors

CAROLINE BARRON is senior lecturer in History at Bedford College, University of London. She has written books and articles on a variety of topics in late medieval English history, but she is particularly interested in the reign of Richard II and the history of London. She is currently working on a map of London as it was before the dissolution of its forty or so religious houses in the late 1530s, and also on a study of the parish fraternities of late medieval London. She is writing a general history of London during the period 1216–1485.

DAVID CARPENTER is lecturer in History at Queen Mary College, University of London. He has published articles on various aspects of English history in the thirteenth century, and is currently working on a biography of King Kenry III to be published by Eyre Methuen in the *Monarchs of England* series.

M.T. CLANCHY is Reader in Medieval History at the University of Glasgow. He has edited legal texts for the Selden Society and the Wiltshire Record Society and is the author of *From Memory to Written Record: England 1066–1272* (1979), and *England and Its Rulers, 1066–1272* (1983). He is working at present on the charters of Durham cathedral and on a study of *Woman and the Book in the Middle Ages*.

ANNE J. DUGGAN is lecturer in History at Queen Mary College, University of London. She has published several articles on Thomas Becket, and a book *Thomas Becket: A Textual History of his Letters* (1980). Her chief academic interests are ecclesiastical, intellectual and cultural history, and her major work to date, *The Correspondence of Thomas Becket, Archbishop of Canterbury*, is close to completion.

JOHN GILLINGHAM is senior lecturer in History at the London School of Economics. His most recent publications are *The Angevin Empire* (1984) and *War and Government in the Middle Ages* (edited with J.C. Holt) (1984). He has published widely and his books include biographies of Richard the Lionheart and Oliver Cromwell, a study of the Wars of the Roses and (with M. Falkus) *The Historical Atlas of Britain*. His current research interest is English and French history in the twelfth and thirteenth centuries.

CHRIS GIVEN-WILSON, lecturer in the Mediaeval History Department, University of St Andrews, was awarded his Ph.D. in 1976 for a thesis on the household of Edward III. He is joint author of two books, *Mediaeval Monasteries of Great Britain*, with Lionel Butler (1979) and *Royal Bastards of England*, with his wife, Alice Curteis (1984), and has published several articles. His major research interest is the English nobility of the fourteenth century and he is currently completing a book on the *English Royal Household 1360–1413*.

ALEXANDER GRANT is a lecturer in History at Lancaster University. He was educated at Dingwall Academy and Oxford University, and taught at Sheffield University and Queen's University, Belfast before moving to Lancaster. He teaches English, Scottish and French medieval history, and his main research interest is the late medieval Scottish nobility, on which he has published several articles. He is also the author of Volume III in the 'New History of Scotland', *Independence and Nationhood: Scotland 1306–1469* (1984).

RICHARD MACKENNEY teaches History at the University of Edinburgh. His research interests centre on the economic, social and political functions of guilds, particularly those of Venice, where he has worked extensively in the State Archives. He has published articles and reviews on Venice and is presently working on a short history of the city and also on a textbook on Europe in the sixteenth century.

GEOFFREY PARKER is Professor of Modern History at the University of St Andrews where he has taught since 1972. He has published several books on European history including *The Army of Flanders and the Spanish Road, 1567–1659* (1972), *The Dutch Revolt* (1977), *Philip II: a biography* (1978), *Spain and the Netherlands, 1559–1659* (1978), *Europe in Crisis, 1598–1648* (1979) and *The Thirty Years War* (1984). His main research interest is the expansion of Europe into the wider world in the sixteenth and seventeenth centuries.

JOHN POST has been an assistant keeper of Public Records since 1975. He has published numerous articles on medieval history, especially on women, criminal law and the uses of medieval records. His current research interests are very wide, encompassing the disadvantaging of women in legal procedure, the usurpation of 1399, jury composition and behaviour and the social functions of castration.

LESLEY M. SMITH, the editor, studied history at the University of St Andrews and Brasenose College, Oxford. She now works as a researcher at London Weekend Television. She has co-edited (with Geoffrey Parker) *The General Crisis of the Seventeenth Century* (1978) and has also edited *The Making of Britain* Vol I, *The Dark Ages*. She is currently researching a book on the history of Britain during the Interregnum.

W.L. WARREN is Professor of Modern History at Queen's University, Belfast. His first major book was on *King John* (1961), followed by *Henry II* (1973) which was awarded a Wolfson Literary Prize in History. He has since been writing on the Normans in Ireland, but his next book will be on medieval English government. He has been Dean of Theology, and a member of the Arts Council of Northern Ireland. He is also a Fellow of the Royal Historical Society and of the Royal Society of Literature, and is a member of the Royal Irish Academy.

Index